HEALTH CARE ARCHITECTURE

DESIGNS FOR THE FUTURE

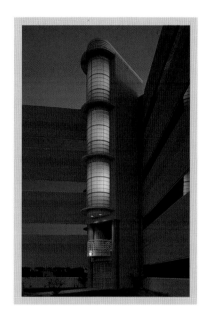

Eleanor Lynn Nesmith

The American Institute of Architects Press
Washington D.C.

First published in the United States of America by:
Rockport Publishers, Inc.
146 Granite Street
Rockport, Massachusetts 01966
Telephone: (508) 546-9590
Fax: (508) 546-7141

Distributed to the book trade and art trade in the U.S. and Canada by:
The AIA Press
1735 New York Avenue
Washington, DC 20006
Telephone: 800-626-ARCH
Fax: 800-678-7102

Other Distribution by:
Rockport Publishers, Inc.
Rockport, Massachusetts 01966

ISBN 1-55835-135-3

10 9 8 7 6 5 4 3 2 1

Art Director: Laura Herrmann
Design Firm: KBB Design
Layout and Production: Kathleen Kelley
Cover Photograph: Jane Lidz

Printed in Hong Kong

DEDICATION

For my father and in memory of my mother

ACKNOWLEDGMENTS

A number of individuals assisted in bringing this book to fruition. First, I would like to thank
all the architects who submitted health care facilities and the numerous architectural photographers who allowed use of their work in this publication. I am also indebted to Jim Jonassen
for writing the foreword and providing information on several projects designed by NBBJ;
the various architects who shared their views on the future direction of the profession;
Michael J. Crosbie for first suggesting the idea of a book on health care architecture;
Allen Freeman and Andrea Oppenheimer Dean for their unfailing and ongoing support;
Donald Canty for providing the perfect environment to launch a career in architectural
journalism; and everybody at Rockport Publishers.

TABLE OF CONTENTS

FOREWORD

By Jim Jonassen, FAIA

Design for future change has been a critical factor in health care architecture for as long as I can remember. The nature of change anticipated in the 1970s and 1980s centered on growth and technologically driven change. In the mid-1980s through the early 1990s the focus in many industrialized countries, with the United States leading the way, became more oriented toward achieving a friendlier environment for the patient. Much of this trend was driven by marketing concepts aimed at attracting patients directly, as well as attracting physicians and staff to an institution. Most of the built projects featured in this book were influenced by these ideas. This is particularly true of the specialty projects, such as cancer centers, pediatric facilities, and women's centers.

Another shift which chronologically overlays the friendly-environment trend, is occuring in the approach to delivering care. This trend arose in an increased emphasis on ambulatory care and less invasive interventions; originally these changes were cost- and convenience-driven. More recently, changes in care delivery have become much broader in focus, aimed at an integration of health care both vertically and horizontally. The outpatient centers and health maintenance organization facilities in this book are excellent illustrations of this trend.

Of course, to the health care deliverer and the health facility architect, the really interesting question is, "Where are health facilities headed next?" This issue is not easily addressed, whether in the U.S. or in the other industrialized nations of the world. Even so, I think there are several overriding principles which should and will shape the coming generation of health care facilities.

Design for Value

The first of these principles is design for optimum value by balancing cost, quality, and access. By this I mean the planning and design of health systems and facilities which most effectively deliver actual and perceived quality care. Someone not familiar with health care delivery might think that this is what has always been done.

But the reality is that health care design has been shaped instead by constraints internal to the industry, such as specialization, as well as by external forces, which have at various

times pulled hard in one of the directions of cost, quality, or access, but never sought all three in balance with affordability. This will mean future health delivery and facility systems will bypass the current paradigms of compartmentalized care and deliver integrated care in friendly environments. New types of facilities will arise to achieve this. Health education, maintenance, and service delivery ·facilities in the workplace, home, and school are good examples. Facilities which integrate inpatient and outpatient reception, such as the University of Rochester Access Center and Ambulatory Care Center, are another example. Campuses which integrate a full continuum of primary ambulatory care through tertiary inpatient care may be one of the more significant new architectural forms. The Genesys Health System Campus in Flint, Michigan is an early example of this approach. The retail pharmacy may also give way to a new type of facility: a multipurpose, aided, self-help health facility, which would be a true shift into retail health care.

Facilities as Tool and Healer

The second principle combines two compatible philosophies: that the physical settings of health care delivery support productivity and effectiveness, and that they are an end in themselves—aiding in the healing and wellness process through psycho-physiological effect. The recently completed project for Riverside Hospital in Columbus, Ohio, was developed specifically to address the spiritual

ABOVE:

A 671,000-square-foot addition to the Swedish Medical Center in Seattle, Washington, is designed by NBBJ to provide a bold new entrance for the facility. The new wing is organized with diagnostic and treatment functions conveniently located near the hospital's new "front door."

aspects of the healing process. Important elements of this approach will include more comprehensive applications of recent research findings on the effects of color, light quality, acoustics, outlook, air quality, and individual control. Better understanding of these issues will influence the emphasis on high-quality spiritual design in heath care facilities.

Green Facilities

The third and final principle that I think will shape our health facilities is the broad concept generally referred to as "greening." This means that health facilities will accept a responsibility to act as role models in enabling a healthy local and global environment. The design effect will be the exercise of great care in the selection of materials and systems that are nontoxic and environmentally sustainable.

These three principles, "Design for Value," "Facilities as Both Tool and Healer," and "Green Facilities," are equally important in any system of health care. They are very powerful forces that will shape future health care architecture.

INTRODUCTION
By Eleanor Lynn Nesmith

Health care delivery is undergoing a dramatic transformation, and the design of medical facilities is beginning to reflect these revolutionary changes. The operational organization and the physical setting of hospitals are in the process of a complete overhaul. Diverse factors—technology, regulatory requirements, codes, social attitudes, reimbursement policies—influence the way health care facilities are programmed, designed, and built. As the complexity of patient care increases, architects also are called upon to devise new models to accommodate advances in medical research and treatment philosophies. In addition, a host of new health care building types are emerging to meet increasingly diverse and specialized client needs.

Architects are key players in shaping future medical settings and ensuring that hospital environments are conducive to the provision of quality care. But in today's competitive marketplace, the design team must also respect the hospital's bottom line. Administrators are placing greater burdens on their planners to rescue them from expensive overgrowth and redundancy. "Accountability is the name of the game," explains architect Brendan Morrisroe of TRO/The Ritchie Organization. "Architects today are called upon to develop a vision for capital investment and tweak out operational enhancements for the health care provider." In addition, the medical establishment is starting to understand that in the long run innovative, functional and spatial relationships can reduce both construction and building life cycle costs.

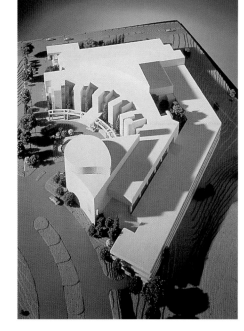

Traditionally, hospitals served as the care givers and custodians of the bedridden. More and more, the acute-care medical center is not the primary provider of health care services. Hospitals are moving away from their traditional roles. The dramatic increase in the number of ambulatory care centers and outpatient care facilities is one of the most significant trends in the health care field.

During the past 10 years, heath care administrators have separated less-expensive outpatient care from their acute-care hospitals. Such outpatient and ambulatory care centers, which usually contain doctors' offices, surgical facilities, and diagnostic and treatment functions, cost significantly less to construct, since they do not need to meet the same strict building codes that govern hospitals. In addition, these facilities can be designed so that ordinary administrative tasks are not performed in the same high-cost space as technology-intensive procedures.

Ambulatory facilities also provide architects with greater opportunity for sensitive and innovative design. Although the needs of outpatient clients might be less complex than those of patients confined to acute-care hospitals, many ambulatory clients are being treated for a life-threatening illness—cancer, AIDS, kidney disease—which often requires repeat visits and serious therapies.

RIGHT AND BELOW:

A new women's clinic, Centro Medico de la Mujer, located in Monterrey, Mexico, will house a medical office building and full inpatient and outpatient services including 50 private patient suites, six delivery rooms, and four operating rooms. HDR is providing programming and schematic design.

Although hospitals are under intense pressure to contain costs, these same institutions are also required to continually improve the quality of care to remain competitive. To meet these diverse challenges, many health care providers have responded with a concept called "patient-focused" or "patient-centered" care. In facilities designed around the needs of the patient, routine diagnoses and treatments are decentralized. The result is the establishment of singular settings in which a coordinated medical team attends to the patient. Instead of shuffling the individual around the hospital, special equipment needed to augment the hospital's built-in services is brought to the bedside. Such decentralization produces operational savings for the institution. Some departments—such as admitting and discharge planning—eventually disappear, as the nursing staff takes responsibility for the care management of individual patients through bedside computing.

To make patients feel more comfortable in a hospital setting, architects are turning increasingly to recognizable building prototypes, such as the shopping mall, as organizational tools. This configuration provides the required framework for a hospital's "centers of excellence" or "clinic campaigns." Accordingly, the hospital is organized by afflictions rather than by departments, and all are located adjacent to one other along a mall-like atrium. In addition to providing the medical center with a stronger image, this arrangement translates into less travel between services for patients and closer proximity for staff.

Advances in pediatric care and an emphasis on specialized treatment for children are shaping new models of health care for young patients. The new pediatric facilities require par-

ticular attention because children are the most vulnerable of patients and are more environmentally sensitive than most adults. In response to these special concerns, architects must explore ways to engage and communicate with these isolated and frightened young patients and include their families in the healing process. Pediatric facilities should be holistically planned so that parents and siblings can be comfortable, and to encourage them to participate in care. Regional hospitals are building freestanding pediatric centers, and sub-building types are emerging, including medically-managed day care for children with AIDS and pediatric trauma centers.

The targeting of special patient groups has also resulted in a burgeoning of women's centers, which house an array of birthing, gynecological, preventive medicine, and educational services. In marketing hospitals, administrators hope specialized centers will engender "hospital brand loyalty" whereby a positive experience during childbirth will carry over to other medical services.

Other new building types are emerging for treating disorders unheard of even a decade ago. Rehabilitation centers for victims of traumatic head injuries are one example of new specialized facilities. Before the advent of high-technology emergency medical care, many victims of such injuries would not have survived the initial shock. These rehabilitation

centers' mission is to involve patients in their own recovery and to provide a physical setting to enhance that goal.

Adaptability and expandability to accommodate new requirements and technological advances are paramount. The whole medical industry seems in a state of flux and one of the biggest challenges facing architects today is the ability to be flexible and to change their paradigms. Medical centers of the future will also make site-related changes as mergers, acquisitions, and consolidations continue to transform the whole health care industry. These administrative restructurings have reduced the number of health care entities, altered hospital management, and affected the procurement of architectural services.

Kaiser Permanente, a national health maintenance organization (HMO) is representative of health care delivery and architecture's new direction. Kaiser Permanente employs its own doctors and staff, and builds and operates its own hospitals and ambulatory care facilities. Kaiser understands the absolute necessity of visionary plans for a building program. "Currently, we are designing all major facilities in three different sizes, which assures us flexibility depending on patient volume," explains Ed Denton, associate director of design for the North California region. In addition, Kaiser requests that architects use established design standards on room layouts and detailed departmental templates.

Architecture provides a critical link between the patient and the health care professional, and the delivery of quality care is often dependent on this relationship. The optimal clinical setting must address and treat not just the medical, but also the emotional, social, and psychological needs of the patient. Sometimes these needs are seemingly contradictory. Hospital architecture with a high-tech image seems to attract patients and instill confidence in the hospital's ability to provide the latest in medical procedures. At the same time, people are attracted to health care environments that are reassuringly familiar. Architects must harness the power of design to create buildings that meet diverse goals and that promote good health and the art of healing.

ABOVE:

Umm Al-Qura University Medical Campus is a teaching facility in Mecca, Saudi Arabia. Designed by Perkins & Will, the new medical complex will include a 400-bed hospital, classrooms, and dormitory space for approximately 1,500 students.

BELOW:

Using a patient-focused philosophy, O'Donnell Wicklund Pigozzi & Peterson designed Rush-Copley Medical Center, a 144-bed replacement hospital.

THE JOHNS HOPKINS OUTPATIENT CENTER

BALTIMORE, MARYLAND

Over the years, Johns Hopkins, like many urban medical centers, has expanded significantly but without a cohesive or comprehensible organization. Payette Associates was hired to remedy the situation through the development of a master plan for the five-block area across the street from the Johns Hopkins' landmark-domed administrative building.

The new 440,000-square-foot outpatient center was organized on the sequence of the "ideal patient visit." This concept established a standard for the layout of clinical spaces. Consulting with nurses, administrators, and physicians throughout the design process, the architects designed the typical floor of the outpatient center in a cluster, with four examination rooms anchoring the four corners of a square plan. This arrangement is an innovative departure from the traditional placement of exam rooms along a linear corridor. The clustered configuration provides each of the corner rooms with additional privacy, and the gateway, or entrance to the cluster, serves as a charting station and stretcher park.

The architects also designed the typical floor as a series of modular units along department lines to increase flexibility and encourage staff to be cross-trained for operational efficiency. A glass greenhouse corridor doubles as a waiting area and provides an orienting circulation pattern.

OPPOSITE:
Clinics are fronted by individual reception areas located along a greenhouse corridor. The architects created separate administration spaces—one for receiving patients and the other for billing/scheduling.

REGISTRATION

LEFT:
Patient registration has been streamlined. Upon arrival, visitors simply check in at main reception desk in the lobby and proceed to the appropriate treatment area.

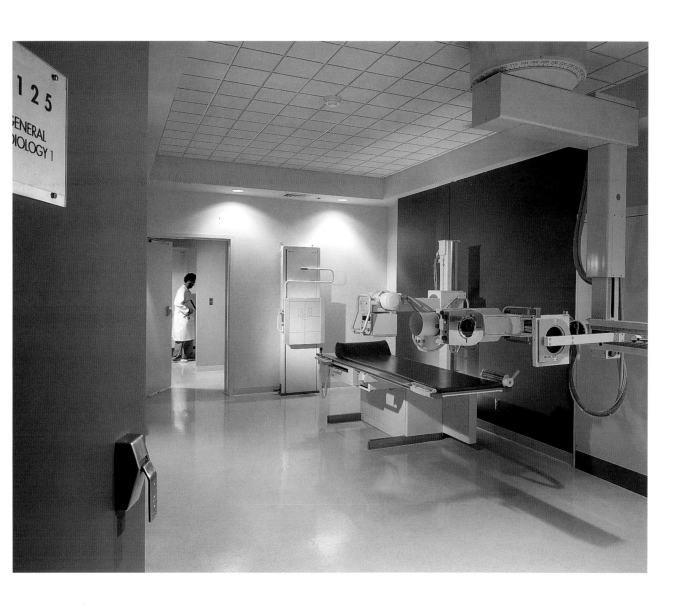

RIGHT:

Payette Associates arranged
the clinical floors in a simple
gridlike configuration with
eight-room clusters.

OPPOSITE:

The eight-story clinic was
designed as a "one-stop" shop
with an array of outpatient
clinical services from all
hospital specialties.

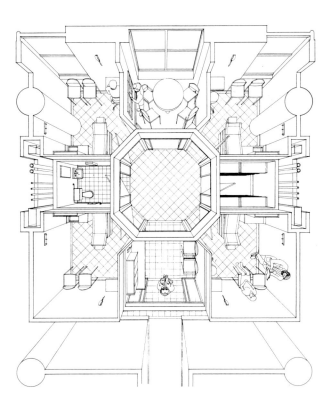

ABOVE:

The walkway continues into the outpatient building as a main concourse, leading to a below-grade pedestrian corridor, which links the new wing to the existing medical complex.

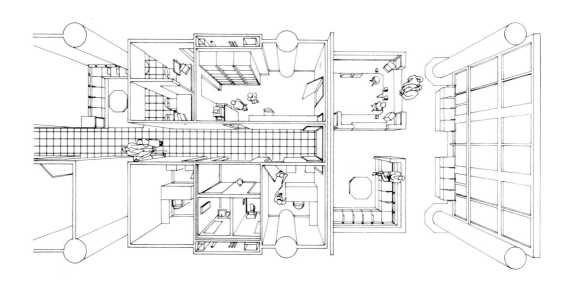

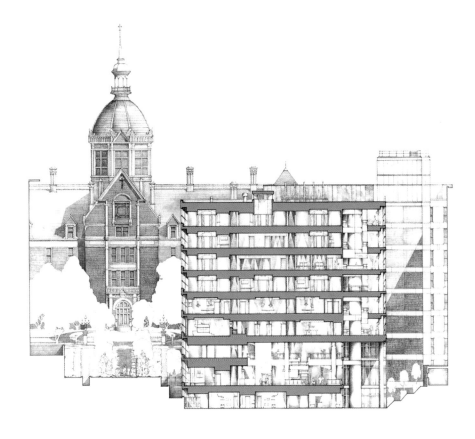

SHILEY EYE CENTER
UNIVERSITY OF CALIFORNIA, SAN DIEGO

SAN DIEGO, CALIFORNIA

Developing new medical delivery systems requires complex and sometimes conflicting design solutions. The University of San Diego's Department of Ophthalmology was experiencing rapid growth and sought to consolidate clinical and research activities that were located in four widely dispersed locations.

Anshen + Allen's design concept was driven by the need to bring together these related but independent functions in a way that reinforces the department as a cohesive whole yet creates a separate identity for the public and private areas. The architects deftly organized the 36,400-square-foot building into discrete clinical and research wings. Anshen + Allen's principal designers

David Rinehart and Jack MacAllister studied under and later worked for Louis Kahn. The Shiley Eye Center reflects Kahn's powerful influence on the designers by the incorporation of simple geometric forms, the concrete-framed stucco finish, the subtle play of natural light, and the skillful use of basic materials to achieve a pristine elegance.

A two-story pavilion, which anchors the northern edge of the site, houses faculty and administrative offices, as well as the library and conference area. Technical spaces, which include examination rooms, laboratories, and an outpatient surgery center, are contained in the larger three-story wing. A glazed circulation spine connects the two components.

ABOVE:
Nontechnical spaces, including the library/conference area and faculty offices, are housed in a two-story wing, which is crowned with a vaulted roof.

OPPOSITE:
Second-story bridges at the end of the glazed corridor join the faculty offices in the vaulted front section of the building with the labs in the back.

RIGHT:
The auditorium features maple paneling with an exposed concrete frame and an elegant, curving ceiling detail.

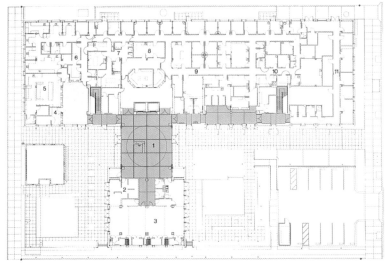

GROUND FLOOR PLAN

AMBULATORY CARE/OUTPATIENT CENTERS

The architects separated public and private functions from circulation in the facility, and provided distinct entrances for the clinical and administration/research departments.

RIGHT:
The faculty office waiting room takes advantage of the vaulted roof form; radiused west-facing windows scoop in sunlight.

ABOVE:
The Eye Center's lobby is enlivened with works of art, composite stone floors, and custom-crafted maple fixtures and furnishings.

TANG CENTER, UNITED HEALTH SERVICE
UNIVERSITY OF CALIFORNIA, BERKELEY

BERKELEY, CALIFORNIA

Universities and colleges are under intense pressure to provide quality health services to students, faculty, and staff. The Tang Center, designed by Anshen + Allen, was built to respond to the rapidly growing requirements of the University of California, Berkeley. This new 75,000-square-foot ambulatory care center replaces the university's dated Cowell Hospital.

Given the university's demanding fast-track schedule, project design and construction were divided into four separate bid packages, which allowed ordering and fabrication of long lead items to be done prior to completion of the full design. Total time from programming to user occupancy was three years.

The Tang Center houses five main functions: medical services; health promotion, a wellness center and occupational health services; psychological services; a conference center; and administration.

The three-story building is comprised of two wings, one for clinical services and one devoted to administrative functions. Designed to meet the strictest of California seismic codes, the facility serves as an earthquake emergency preparedness center for the county. A central atrium lobby links the facility's two components. The main public corridors feature views out to a series of landscaped courtyards interspersed between the angled wings. This configuration also allows for future expansion without altering the overall circulation patterns.

ABOVE:

The central atrium opens onto public corridors on each floor with views to courtyards and entrances to clinical departments.

ABOVE:
The architects ringed the lobby atrium with balconies and tucked intimate waiting areas into the corners.

LEFT:
A glass atrium rising three stories high links the facility's two wings.

AMBULATORY CARE/OUTPATIENT CENTERS

ABOVE:

Landscaped courtyards with clustered seating areas provide a strong indoor-outdoor relationship.

UNIVERSITY OF NEBRASKA MEDICAL CENTER, OUTPATIENT CARE CENTER

OMAHA, NEBRASKA

In recent years, health care providers have seized the opportunity to provide less expensive outpatient care by consolidating ambulatory care services and building new wings or freestanding facilities within the existing hospital complex. Hansen Lind Meyer's new $26 million Outpatient Care Center for the University of Nebraska meets this goal and provides a new circulation pattern and unifying order to the sprawling medical complex.

In deference to the old hospital's red brick and precast concrete exterior, HLM repeated these same materials but crafted them in a fresh and contemporary manner. With approximately two-thirds of patients using the hospital on an outpatient basis, it made sense to relocate the institution's main entrance in the new clinic. A curving glass

canopy marks the new vehicular drop-off and approach and reinforces one's feeling of arrival.

Designed to accommodate more than 200,000 patient visits per year, the new facility houses eight ambulatory clinics, inpatient surgery, radiology, a pharmacy and gift shop, medical records, and a new public lobby. Visitors to the Outpatient Center move through the canopy to a bright and airy three-story reception area. The architects used geometric forms, visual cues, and prominent signage to create a logical wayfinding pattern throughout the entire complex. As well, prominently located escalators along the main pedestrian circulation route help reduce the passenger loads on the elevator system.

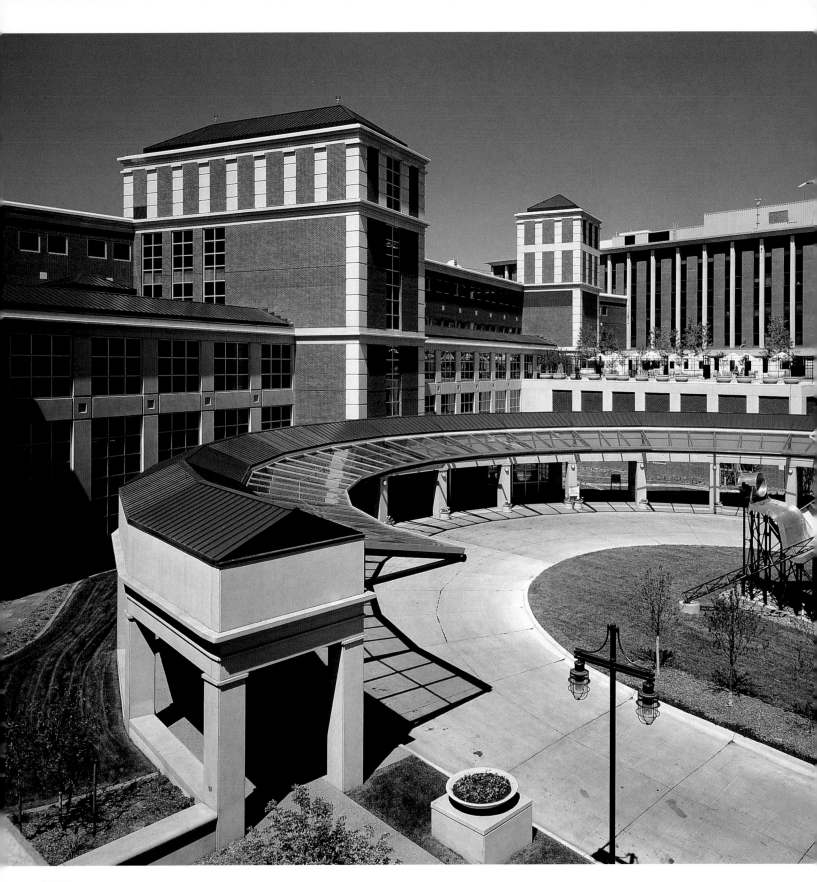

ABOVE:

With a projection of more than 200,000 annual outpatient visits, the architects gave the center a prominent and identifiable ceremonial entrance, incorporating a new circular vehicle drop-out.

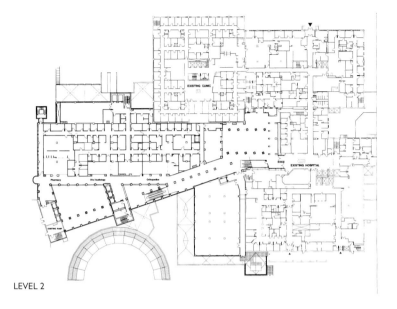

LEVEL 2

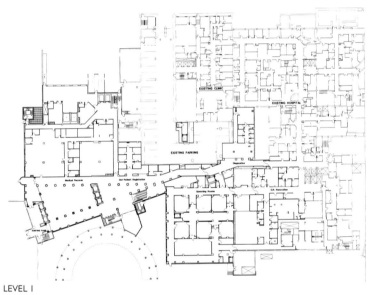

LEVEL 1

RIGHT:
Architectural details,
fabric-covered walls, and
warm colors humanize the
Center's nurses' stations
and waiting areas.

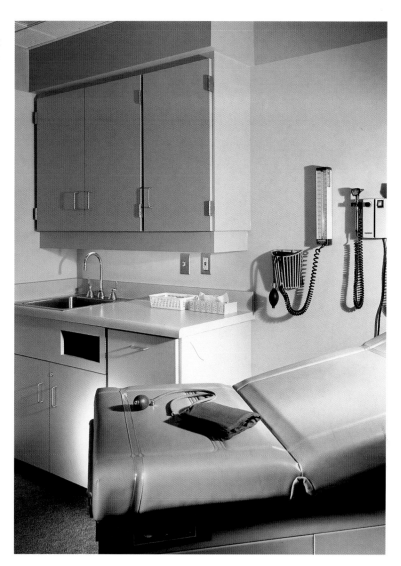

RIGHT:
The Center is organized along
a modular design with examination rooms and clinical
spaces that can be adapted
for flexibility.

LEFT:
Each end of the Center is
anchored with a three-story
atrium. Escalators reduce
passenger load on the
elevators and improve
patient/visitor wayfinding.

UNIVERSITY OF NORTH CAROLINA
AMBULATORY CARE CENTER

CHAPEL HILL, NORTH CAROLINA

Located on the edge of the UNC School of Medicine, this ambulatory care center, designed by Ellerbe Becket, houses the faculty practice for day surgery, ophthalmology, rheumatology/orthopedic surgery, obstetrics and gynecology, dermatology, psychiatry, general medicine, and limited diagnostic services.

The 130,000-square-foot building is the first of three anticipated phases for ambulatory care at the medical school, allowing the university to meet the ever-increasing demand for outpatient services. Architects Ellerbe Becket sited the facility to respond to both the initial and future phases. Clear entrance and approach routes allow easy access to the facility. The design follows existing access to achieve major public entrances on two floors, each handicapped accessible, and to allow parking to be dispersed around the building, thus minimizing travel distances.

The plan for each of the three floors provides flexible and modular space to serve the patient care, research, and teaching requirements of the program. Each public entrance leads to a central reception area and vertical circulation core. Each clinic area is monitored from the main reception area, and a loop circulation pattern in each module permits planning flexibility as program requirements change.

Designed as a transition between the medical school and the surrounding residential neighborhoods, the facility uses forms and materials that recall the character of campus architecture, and the scale of the stepped plan, entrances, and fenestration pattern creates an inviting, friendly environment.

ABOVE:

At night, the large windows along the building's facade create a warm and inviting environment.

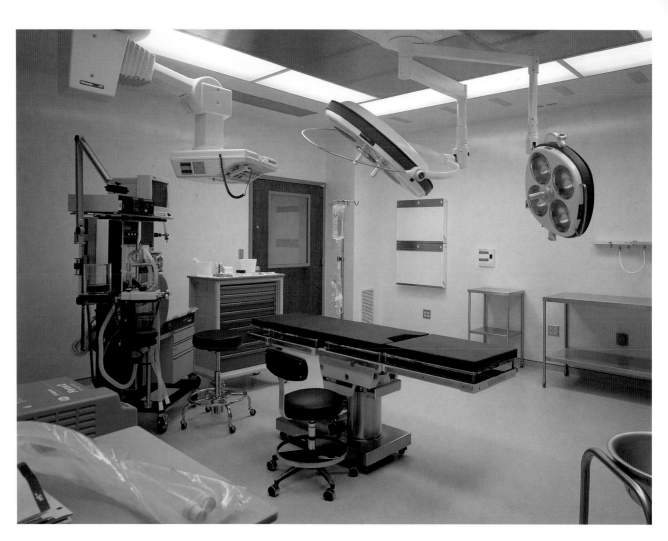

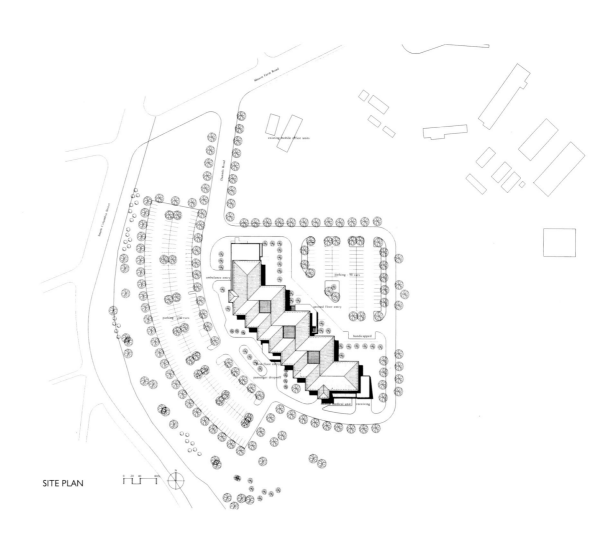

SITE PLAN

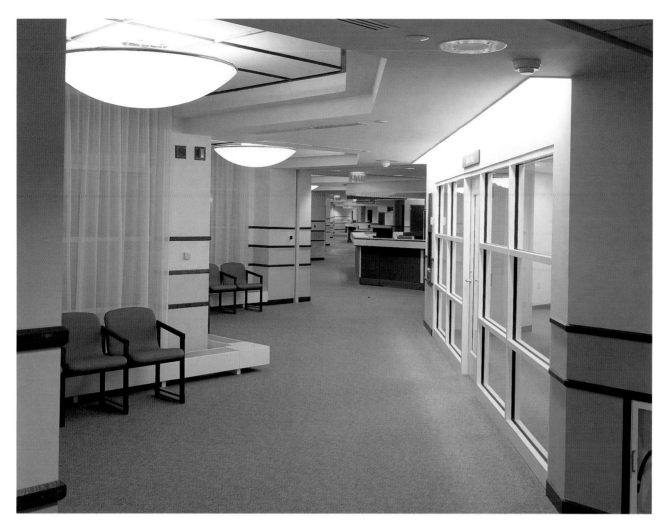

ABOVE:

The Ambulatory Care Center is organized with a loop circulation pattern and a series of intimate waiting areas tucked within the zigzag of the stepped floor plan.

SAINT FRANCIS HOSPITAL CANCER CENTER

HARTFORD, CONNECTICUT

Recognizing the unsettling nature of the oncology therapy experience, TRO/The Ritchie Organization designed this 31,200-square-foot freestanding Cancer Center to meet the functional requirements of a high-tech medical facility while creating a healing environment that is emotionally reassuring.

The architects used natural materials for both exterior and interior finishes and incorporated large windows in the waiting and treatment rooms. A double-height, glazed entry rotunda with its cable-suspended glass canopy marks the new oncology center and houses a generously proportioned reception area. From the lobby, patients and families can view the formal forecourt and the landscaped grounds of the campus.

Within the radiation therapy and simulator rooms, the architects incorporated colorful wall murals which depict the changing seasons. Departmental adjacencies and the grouping of similar services create operational efficiency and space-planning economy. Clear orientation and circulation patterns increase staff observation and response time to patients in need.

The Cancer Center is the first completed component of a long-term, $132 million modernization program for the entire Saint Francis Hospital complex. In response to a comprehensive master plan, the Cancer Center was sited to define a new edge to the hospital's entry forecourt and the entire medical campus. A new 10-story patient care tower is under construction.

OPPOSITE:

A skewed corridor is set behind a screen wall and serves as the main circulation path. A stairway anchors the southern terminus of the hallway.

ABOVE AND OPPOSITE:

Custom furnishings, textured
fabrics, warm colors, and wood
finishes deinstitutionalize public
spaces and waiting areas.

SYLVESTER COMPREHENSIVE CANCER CENTER
UNIVERSITY OF MIAMI SCHOOL OF MEDICINE

MIAMI, FLORIDA

As diagnostic and treatment procedures become more specialized, major medical centers are building freestanding facilities devoted to specific afflictions. The University of Miami's Sylvester Cancer Center by Payette Associates represents this trend. The new 120,000-square-foot Cancer Center is the first building of a master plan that will eventually expand the school's teaching, research, and clinical capabilities. The complex also includes an outpatient residence called the Hope Lodge, which is co-sponsored by the American Cancer Society.

Drawing from the region's architectural traditions and environmental concerns, Payette Associates organized the facility as a series of three- to six-story stucco structures that provide a new gateway to the medical campus. The design responds to the region's architectural diversity— including Mediterranean, Caribbean, and Moorish influences—and to local climate and environmental forces acting upon the site.

Rejecting the sterile clinical look of old cancer wards, the architects designed attractive public waiting areas and treatment spaces. The main lobby features large windows and residential fixtures and furnishings. A central landscaped courtyard serves as the hub of activity and as an "outdoor living room" for patients and staff. An arcade runs along the courtyard, connecting the cancer clinic to the main hospital.

ABOVE:

The Cancer Center with its formal symmetrical entrance is set back to create a landscaped forecourt that gives a sense of repose.

RIGHT:

Taking advantage of Florida's climate, the two- level arcade provides space for respite and serves as a main pedestrian corridor.

OPPOSITE AND ABOVE:

A colonnade along the east
elevation of the Cancer
Center defines the courtyard
and connects the facility with
the existing hospital.

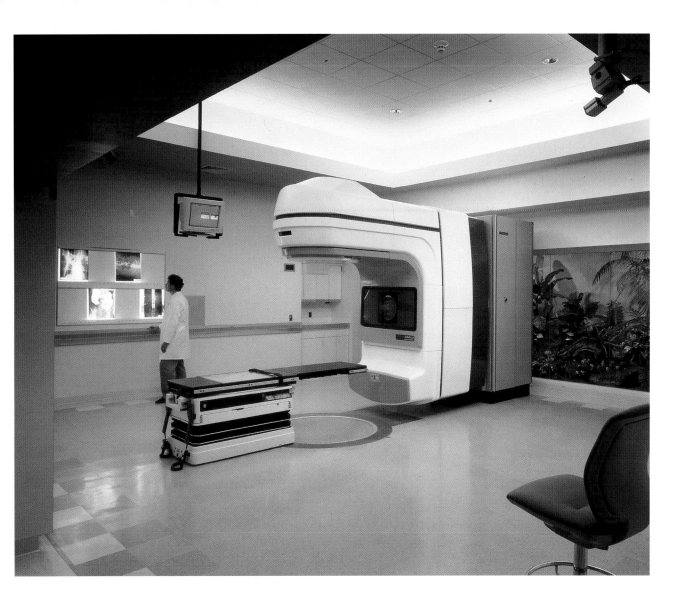

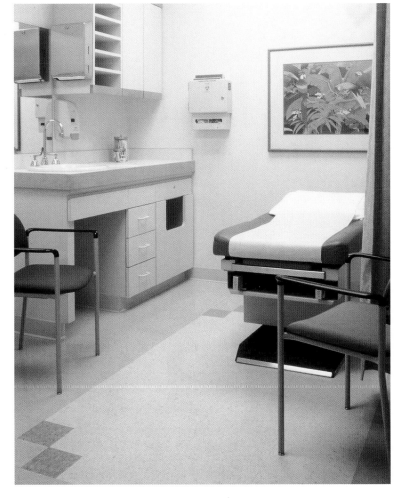

LEFT AND ABOVE:

The Center supports the most technically advanced therapies and houses the latest equipment, including three linear accelerators and two treatment planning simulators.

ABOVE:

In the Sylvester Cancer Center's main lobby, floor-to-ceiling windows flood the space with natural light. A U-shaped, elaborately detailed stairway crafted of polished stone and metals, serves as a linkage between two main floors.

METHODIST CANCER CENTER
NEBRASKA METHODIST HOSPITAL

OMAHA, NEBRASKA

Built as an addition to the Nebraska Methodist Hospital complex, this 52,000-square-foot Cancer Center, designed by HDR, consolidates diagnostic, treatment, therapy, education, and follow-up services in a new outpatient setting with a separate entrance and a unique identity.

The three-story structure is clad in precast concrete similar in color and texture to the adjacent hospital. Curved glass curtain walls along the entrance and north elevation create a spirited exterior facade. A canted-wall auditorium anchors the northeast corner of the site. The architects crowned the auditorium with an illuminated, cylindrical armature, which serves as the facility's symbolic "lighthouse" in the understanding of cancer. The Center's main lobby features a pyramidal skylight with a glass-railed opening on the third floor.

The Cancer Center houses specialty clinical and treatment departments, laboratories, pharmaceutical services, and rehabilitation. Outpatient chemotherapy treatment areas are furnished with recliners, TVs, and VCRs to create the most comfortable environment for the patients. Education and support services are a major component of the facility, including a cancer resource library for patients and families and a 105-seat auditorium which hosts a variety of cancer-related programs. Home health care supervision, financial management advice, family counseling, and chaplain care also are offered at the Cancer Center.

ABOVE:

The Cancer Center imparts a bold new image for the Methodist Hospital complex with its corner auditorium anchoring the facility's northeast boundary.

At night, the new Cancer Center appears like a beacon with its illuminated tower carrying the hospital's logo perched atop the auditorium.

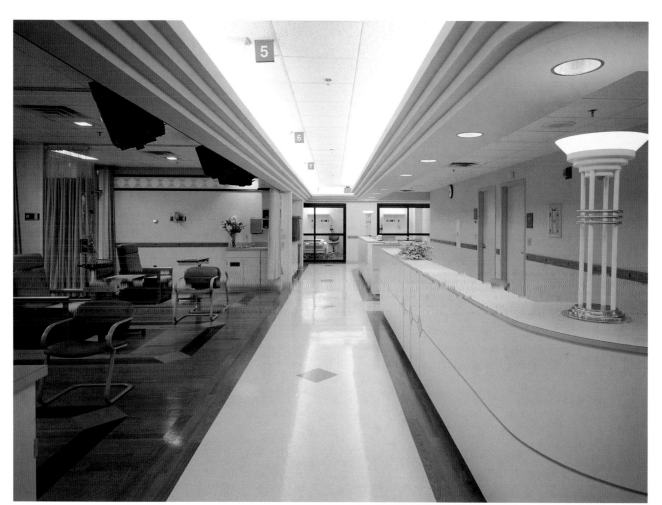

RIGHT:
The infusion area features vinyl bond wood flooring and large windows with views out to a forest.

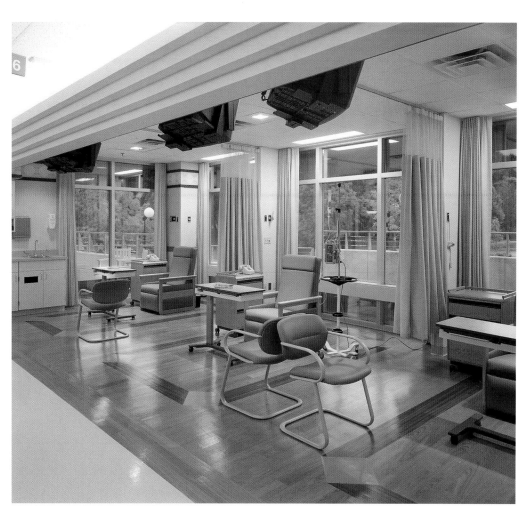

LEFT:
Upper level of the central elevator lobby is crowned with a six-sided skylight. Physician offices are arranged around this public space.

KAISER PERMANENTE MEDICAL CAMPUS

FRESNO, CALIFORNIA

One of the most respected health maintenance organizations, Kaiser Permanente often is cited as a model for managed health care. Although Kaiser's emphasis is on providing quality medical services, the company also understands the importance of physical planning and architecture in delivering quality care.

As part of this push for consistent design quality for new facilities, Kaiser established architectural guidelines which include consistent programming and functional adjacencies based on standardized floor plan templates. For the Kaiser Fresno medical complex, the Ratcliff Architects deviated only slightly from the company's standard template.

The 205,000-square-foot facility was designed as an expandable, three-part complex: treatment areas are located in a series of clinical "pods." A glazed "mall," housed with pharmacies, an optical and eye care store, a cafeteria, and landscaped courtyards, and an ancillary building containing diagnostic and treatment functions, make up the pods. These discrete pods are set at 45-degree angles along a glazed corridor which adjoins an L-shaped support building. This configuration provides efficient circulation patterns and allows for future expansion with minimal interruption of service.

Kaiser's design guidelines allow for a range of interior finishes and furnishings. The courtyard's paving stones and the floating maple panels in the entrance lobby were created by a local craftsperson.

RIGHT:
The highly articulated stucco
and glass facade of new
Fresno medical center reflects
Kaiser's commitment to
state-of-the-art facilities and
services.

RIGHT:
The complex is designed to
accommodate expansion and
flexibility, and an adjoining
200,000-square-foot inpatient
hospital is under construction.

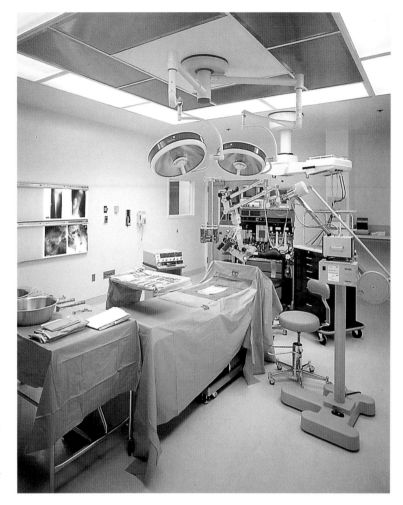

ABOVE:

Critical junctures between the support building and the clustered medical office "pods" are marked with cylindrical columns, recessed ceiling details, and wood panels.

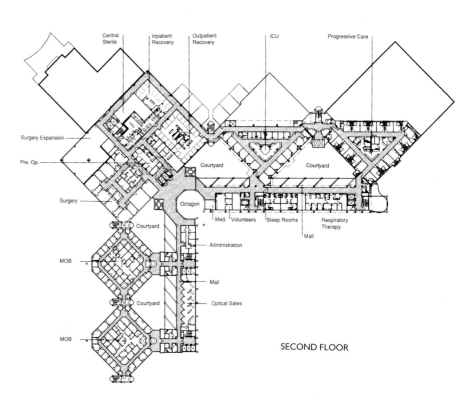

Central Sterile
Inpatient Recovery
Outpatient Recovery
ICU
Progressive Care
Surgery Expansion
Pre. Op.
Courtyard
Courtyard
Surgery
Octagon
Med. Volunteers
Sleep Rooms
Respiratory Therapy
Courtyard
Mall
Administration
MOB
Mall
Courtyard
Optical Sales
MOB

SECOND FLOOR

Photo: © Mark Darley/Esto

KAISER PERMANENTE MEDICAL OFFICE BUILDING

VALLEJO, CALIFORNIA

Economic realities are forcing the health care industry to reevaluate long-held assumptions about the physical setting for the delivery of services. Kaiser Permanente maintains that patients now have more options. When given the choice between more than one provider, many factors come into the decision-making process, including the design and accessibility of clinical facilities. For Kaiser's Vallejo medical office building, Skidmore, Owings & Merrill used an innovative plan, economical materials, and appropriate details to create a reassuring and inviting environment.

Because it is psychologically healing and despite budgetary constraints, the architects brought a maximum of sunlight indoors through generously glazed single-loaded corridors, which also provide views to a series of landscaped courtyards. As well, the 160,000-square-foot office building is composed of 24 standardized modules connected by a central circulation spine. Each two-story modular component is customized to accommodate the needs of each particular clinical specialty.

The architects arranged the facility's 144 physician offices and public waiting areas around landscaped courtyards. To alleviate the disorientation and anxiety of patients entering an unfamiliar facility, public circulation and waiting rooms feature outdoor views. The architects also incorporated double-height lobbies with open stairways and bridges to help orient patients in wayfinding.

ABOVE:

The goal of this new medical facility was to provide an appealing, humanistic institution while meeting operational efficiencies that are critical in the delivery of health services. The two-story building is arranged as a series of modular wings around landscaped courtyards.

RIGHT:

The facility houses approximately 300 modular examination rooms. Straightforward materials were used in a simple yet pleasing arrangement to reduce the stress of the clinical encounter.

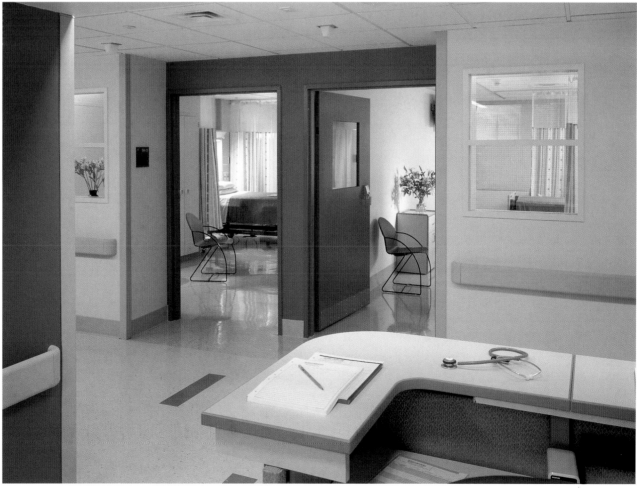

EVERGREEN HOSPICE CENTER

KIRKLAND, WASHINGTON

Although subject to the same strict technical requirements as a hospital, the Evergreen Hospice Center was designed by Seattle architects Mahlum & Nordfors McKinley Gordon to create a noninstitutional facility with the physical and spiritual comforts of home. The Hospice is comprised of four, residentially scaled wings with steeply pitched roofs. Each patient room is expressed on the exterior as a single dormer with double-hung windows.

The approach to the Hospice is along a winding pathway, and the entrance lobby resembles a typical residential living room. Patient rooms are clustered so that they share a "family" room and kitchen. The architects also designed the facility to accommodate social and therapeutic functions, which are not usually incorporated in traditional hospital settings. The grounds feature flower beds for gardening, and patient rooms allow for live-in dogs and cats. The facility's "reflection room" features full-height windows that overlook a semiprivate garden outlined with a circle of aspen trees. Built-in window seats are designed to allow patients to get as close as possible to the out-of-doors in public areas.

The Hospice is organized around a central landscaped courtyard, which has a running stream and a reflecting pool. A single-loaded corridor encircles the garden and provides indoor and outdoor interaction for the patients.

ABOVE:

Stone pavers, colonnades, a bridge, and even a little doghouse enliven the central courtyard, which serves as a focal point for patient activity.

ABOVE:

A family kitchen is located at each wing's entrance to establish a "side door" for informal gatherings, like sharing a cup of coffee or a special meal.

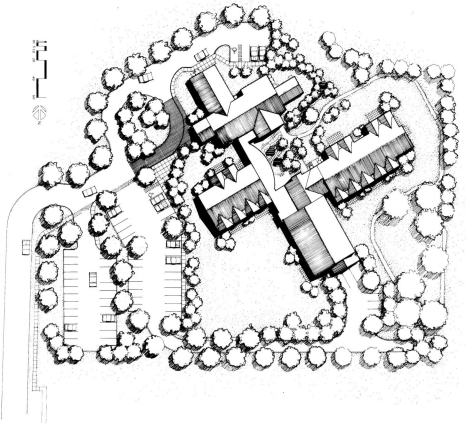

RIGHT:
The Hospice includes a patient
hygiene room for special care
such as massage, hair washing,
and Jacuzzi bathing.

CENTRAL WASHINGTON HOSPITAL

WENATCHEE, WASHINGTON

Over the past 30 years, Central Washington Hospital has grown dramatically, expanding from 40 beds to 176 beds on a rambling medical campus. NBBJ was recently commissioned to expand the emergency department, add a day surgery wing, develop a 22-bed emotional care unit, and add a six-bed pediatric wing. This major expansion also provided an opportunity to establish a sophisticated identity for the regional hospital, which serves a four-county area.

NBBJ's scheme focuses on three, 34-foot-tall screen walls that boldly announce each of the new entrances. These new additions impart a strong image for the facility. Since the region is considered to be the "apple capital" of the world, stucco entry walls were rendered to reflect the colors of the fruit grown in irrigated orchards along the nearby Columbia River Valley: Red Delicious for the emergency wing, Granny Smith green for short-term surgery, and peach for the main entrance. These billboardlike grids also serve as structural supports for new canopies that shelter each entry.

The 9,500-square-foot, short-stay surgery wing accommodates the growing number of outpatient procedures. Single-bed patient recovery rooms ring two interior landscaped courtyards, and nurses' stations are organized around a circular rotunda space. For the new emergency wing, the architects again used a diagonal entry wall to create a congenial, sunlit lobby and tucked the ambulance port behind a stucco wall to screen arriving trauma patients. Although the emergency facility is separated from the hospital by a 25-foot courtyard, the two structures are linked by glass-enclosed corridors.

RIGHT:
Fiberglass canopy provides a
protected shelter at the emergency wing's drop off area.

ABOVE:
Lobbies in the new day
surgery wing feature
18-foot-tall window walls.

OPPOSITE:
Nurses' stations are located in
a rotunda in the center of the
day surgery wing.

ABOVE:

Hospital additions form a pinwheel plan with
color-coded screen walls to announce entrances.
An apple green wall announces the day surgery wing;
a bright red wall marks the new emergency unit.

ABOVE:

A curving wall of clear, aluminum-framed glass defines an 18-foot-high lobby in the new day surgery wing.

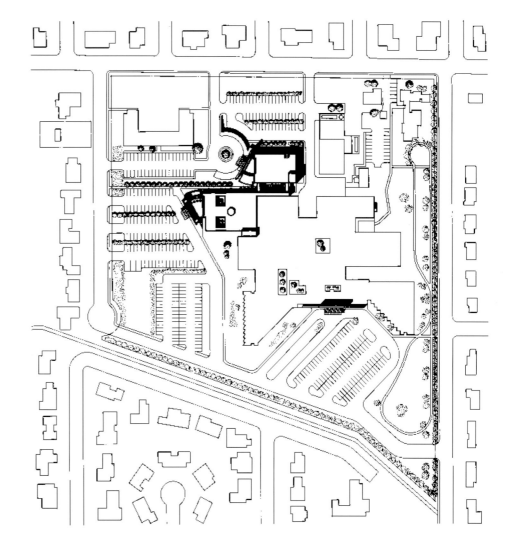

MEDICAL CENTERS

OPPOSITE AND ABOVE:
The architects inserted an
eight-foot gap between the
apple green stucco screen
wall and lobby of the day
surgery unit.

Photo: © Peter Aaron/Esto

COLUMBUS REGIONAL HOSPITAL

COLUMBUS, INDIANA

The small midwestern town of Columbus, Indiana, under the leadership of the Cummins Engine Foundation, is one of the most architecturally sophisticated communities in the United States. Following this tradition of design excellence, Robert A. M. Stern Architects was selected to plan a major expansion and renovation program for the Columbus Regional Hospital.

The medical complex had grown in a haphazard fashion over the past 75 years. To impart order to the 38-acre medical campus, the architects reoriented the hospital toward the Haw Creek, which runs through the parklike site. A new tree-lined approach road with a bridge spanning the creek provides a strong image for the expanded medical center. Flanking the drive are two new 30,000-

square-foot medical office buildings, which act as gatehouses for the complex.

For the existing hospital, the scheme provided for the renovation of a 1917 Italianate-style patient tower. The architects added a series of two-story buildings along landscaped courtyards. These new medical pavilions, each with its own individual identity, are self-contained facilities for cancer care, occupational therapy, intensive care, and a women's center. Continuous double-height galleries connect the new wings, and the hospital restaurant's wide French doors open onto an outdoor dining terrace to provide a welcoming activity center adjacent to the hospital's "front door."

ABOVE:

An existing, six-story patient tower was renovated, including an internal modernization, the addition of a mechanical attic, and a complete exterior recladding.

76 **MEDICAL CENTERS**

Photo: © Peter Aaron/Esto

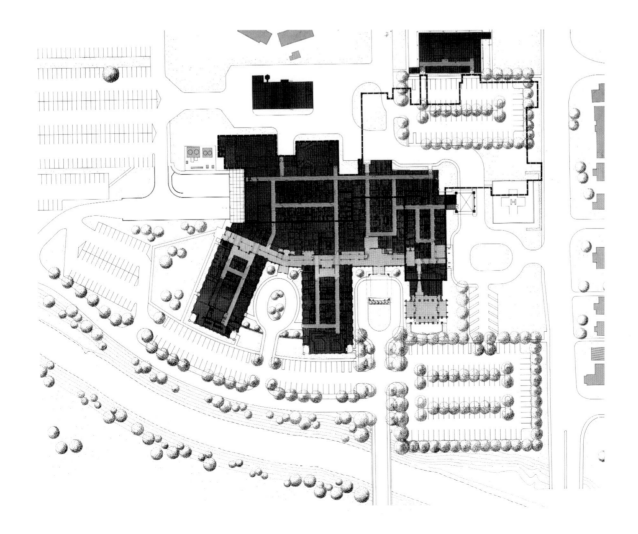

LEFT:

The extensively glazed, double-height concourse contains registration and admitting desks, a gift shop, and waiting areas for various departments.

BELOW:

Taking cues from hotel design, public areas present a welcoming environment.

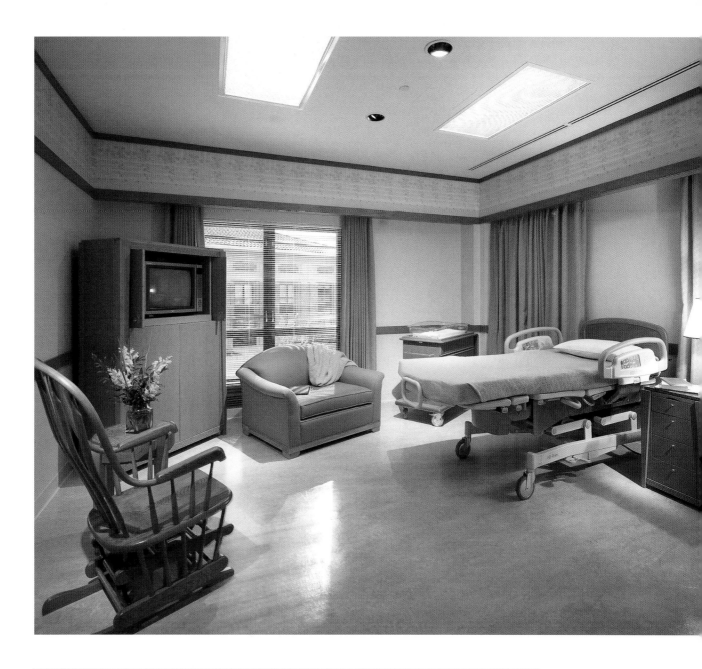

ABOVE:
Patient rooms throughout the acute-care medical facility repeat the warm textures and wood finishes of public areas.

LEFT:
Nursing stations throughout utilize arts-and-craft details in wood ornamentation.

DARTMOUTH-HITCHCOCK MEDICAL CENTER

LEBANON, NEW HAMPSHIRE

Located on a 225-acre wooded site, the Dartmouth-Hitchcock Medical Center was designed by Boston architects Shepley Bulfinch Richardson and Abbott. It comprises a 328-bed inpatient facility made up of twin octagonal towers, a diagnostic and treatment wing, and an ambulatory care center with clinical offices for 160 physicians. Like many new health care facilities, the Dartmouth-Hitchcock complex is designed for future expansion. A freestanding 200,000-square-foot research building is separated from the main complex by a vacant parcel of land reserved for the Dartmouth Medical School.

The architects organized the sprawling 1.1-million-square-foot complex as a linear progression of adjoining low-rise structures along a 390-foot-long atrium mall. This skylit, three-story thoroughfare imparts order and creates an efficient circulation system. A series of 30-foot bays provides rhythm and scale to the space, and the west wall steps back on three levels to admit more natural light.

Among other benefits, this configuration provides the necessary framework for Dartmouth-Hitchcock's "clinical campaigns," a patient-oriented organizational scheme. According to this concept, the facility is organized by patient afflictions rather than by department. In addition to providing a more distinct public identity, the campaigns translate into less movement between services for patients and less travel between bedside and office for staff.

ABOVE:

The complex's main entrance is clearly marked with a 70-foot-tall glass-domed rotunda. From its apex, a series of stepped, skylit A-frame enclosures greet visitors. Glass-enclosed stairwells anchor either end.

OPPOSITE:

The street is flanked by shops, restaurants, and other medical and nonmedical services, and culminates in a 70-foot-high rotunda that serves as an entrance to the entire complex.

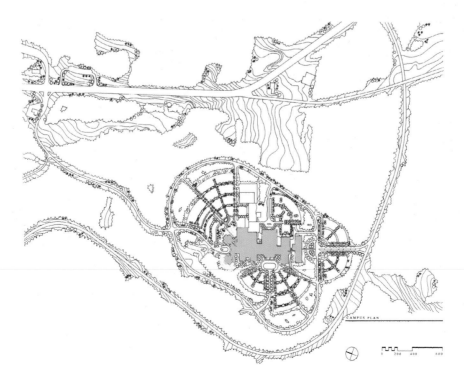

CAMPUS PLAN

LEFT:

The pediatric floor is divided into three separate groups. All patient rooms open onto a series of open play/activities areas.

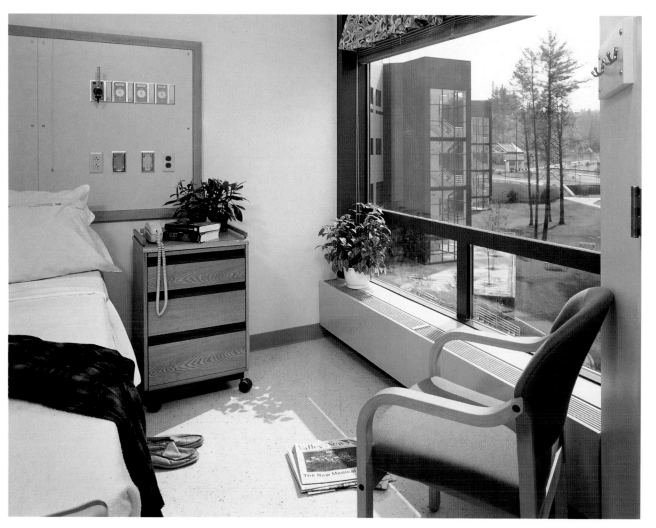

LEFT:

Patient rooms form podlike clusters to provide maximum efficiency for the nursing units and to allow views to the out-of-doors.

LEFT:

This 70-foot-tall rotunda is located directly off the medical center's main entrance and is anchored by an information desk. The medical center is organized horizontally by clinical campaigns and grouped together by floor.

GREATER BALTIMORE MEDICAL CENTER

BALTIMORE, MARYLAND

The Obstetrics/Acute Care expansion by RTKL is the first major inpatient clinical addition to the Greater Baltimore Medical Center since the local firm designed the original hospital 30 years ago. The expansion consists of 180,000 square feet of new construction to house critical care and diagnostic services and 100,000 square feet of renovations. The building program also includes a new gate house, a storm water management pond designed as an urban wildlife sanctuary, and a 950-car parking structure.

To relate new to old while creating a stronger image for the hospital, RTKL divided the addition into two discrete pavilions, linked by an interior courtyard. The building's exterior expression and use of concrete trellises reduce the apparent mass of the new six-story addition and make it compatible with the existing hospital.

The facility is arranged by floor-by-floor clinical focus areas. This configuration increases operational adjacencies and efficiencies. The largest component is a nursing pavilion with cardiac, medical, and surgery units on the upper three floors, all set atop the showpiece of the facility—the new women's birthing center—which is located on the ground floor.

Between the two new wings lies a skylit and balconied atrium courtyard that serves as the principal public space for the women's center. Anchoring the west end of the atrium spine is a glazed lobby that rises the height of the facility. RTKL's use of traditional materials, details, finishes, and daylight all contribute to reducing the scale and the impersonality that often accompanies institutional spaces.

EAST ELEVATION

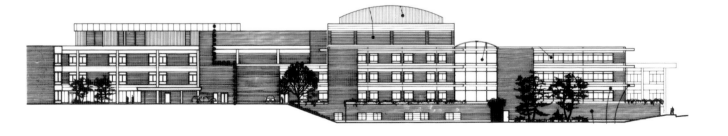

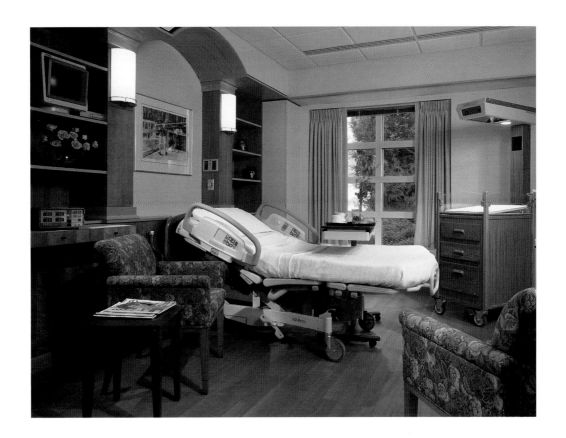

ABOVE:
The natural woods and warm finishes of public spaces are repeated in the LDR rooms. The head wall is fitted with oak-trimmed cherry cabinetry enlivened with a central arch.

RIGHT:
Corridors feature wooden hand railings and textured surfaces in soft colors.

OPPOSITE:
An elegant wood-encased stairway rises in the lobby near the new entrance and serves as an important organizing element.

MCLAREN REGIONAL MEDICAL CENTER

FLINT, MICHIGAN

Perkins & Will developed a phased construction program for the McLaren Regional Medical Center that would allow for continuous operation with minimal disruptions and meet the institution's tight budget.

Located on a tight urban site, the original medical center suffered from a severely cramped ancillary service core, which had been originally constructed in the 1950s to serve a significantly smaller facility. To expedite the construction schedule, a "fast track" building program was developed, which provided for separate bidding processes for the initial package, structure, exterior finishes, and interior finishes. In addition, Perkins & Will designed a lightweight steel structure, which could be fabricated faster than a concrete system.

The architects designed a new nine-story patient tower to rise above the existing four-story base of the original hospital. The 185,200-square-foot addition, which provides technically advanced support services, houses 238 patient beds, an expanded emergency room, an outpatient clinic, and a rehabilitation center. The new tower also houses a women's health center with 14 LDRP suites and four postpartum rooms.

The phased renovation program for the existing hospital also expanded the emergency room and outpatient clinic, which includes ambulatory surgery, physical therapy, speech audiology, and preadmission testing.

RIGHT:

Curved surfaces combined
with warm colors create a
crisp yet inviting atmosphere
on patient floors.

RIGHT:

A new central elevator lobby
provides needed vertical
circulation for the new
patient tower.

NEW BOSTON CITY HOSPITAL

BOSTON, MASSACHUSETTS

Affiliated with Boston's major medical schools, Boston City Hospital is considered one of the foremost teaching hospitals in the country. Although it has a tradition of medical "firsts," the existing facility is antiquated: it was built based on a physical model of health care delivery from the turn of the century.

Hoskins Scott & Partners/Cannon Architects developed a master plan for the urban institution to meet the latest in medical technology in a building with distinctive architectural character. The new 349,000-square-foot complex contains 356 acute-care beds, a trauma center/emergency room, satellite radiology, maternal center, laboratories, and comprehensive medical support functions. Several of the hospital's original buildings have been renovated and integrated to create a cohesive urban campus.

Scale, planning, and materials were selected to blend with the historic neighborhood. The exterior is clad in brick enlivened with a variegated pattern and precast concrete accents. The architects' master plan also provided for extensive landscaping of the entire medical complex. Inside the skylit reception lobby, the architects repeated the detailed brick pattern for walls and floors. Materials, finishes, and furnishings throughout the hospital offer diverse and interesting textural experiences while meeting stringent building codes and maintenance requirements.

ABOVE:

The New Boston City Hospital was designed to create a friendly and inviting ambiance. The skylit entrance lobby repeats the variegated brick pattern of the exterior of the building.

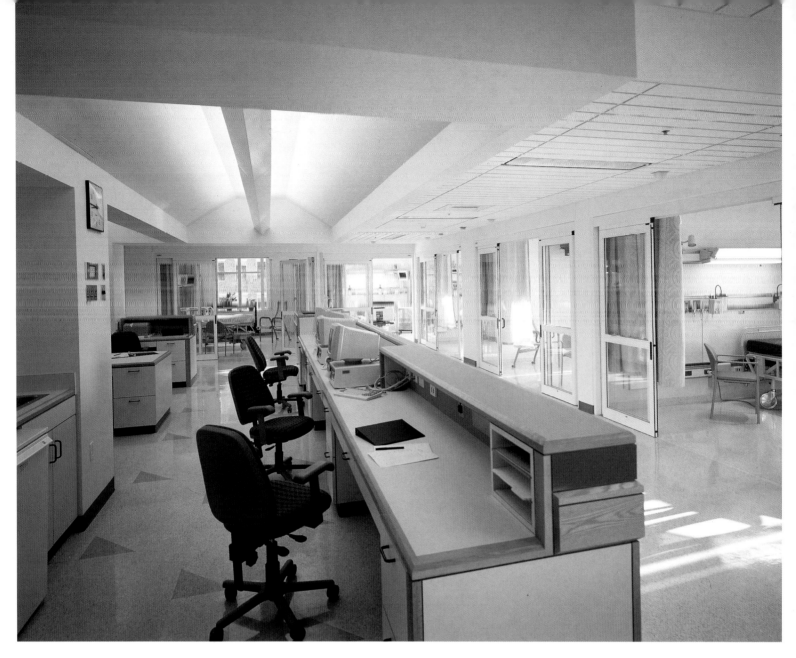

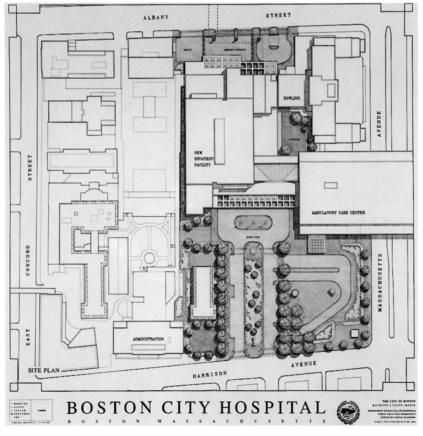

ST. LUKE'S MEDICAL TOWER

HOUSTON, TEXAS

Reflecting the spirit and character of Houston's contemporary architecture, St. Luke's Medical Tower is a sophisticated and innovative medical facility and teaching hospital. The twin octagonal towers straddle the block between two busy city streets and present a dual frontage to define the urban environment. Designed by Cesar Pelli & Associates, the 500,000-square-foot St. Luke's Tower is clad in silver reflective glass detailed with white metal mullions, cornice rails, and a pair of matching spires.

Behind the mirrored-glass skin, the building's precast and cast-in-place concrete structural frame is divided into four sections: six levels of parking set atop a two-story recep-

tion area and three levels below; medical and ambulatory care on floors 9–11; physicians' offices on floors 12–27; and circular roof armatures that screen mechanical equipment. Each section is highly articulated: the second floor extends along both street elevations to create a pedestrian-scaled canopy that ties the new tower to the existing medical complex.

In contrast to the building's gleaming exterior, the building's interiors are paneled in cherry wood and marble and exude warmth and hospitality, avoiding the sterility of many medical settings.

OPPOSITE:
Bold geometrical forms, a sleek curtain wall, and twin spires set St. Luke's Tower apart from the rest of the Texas Medical Center.

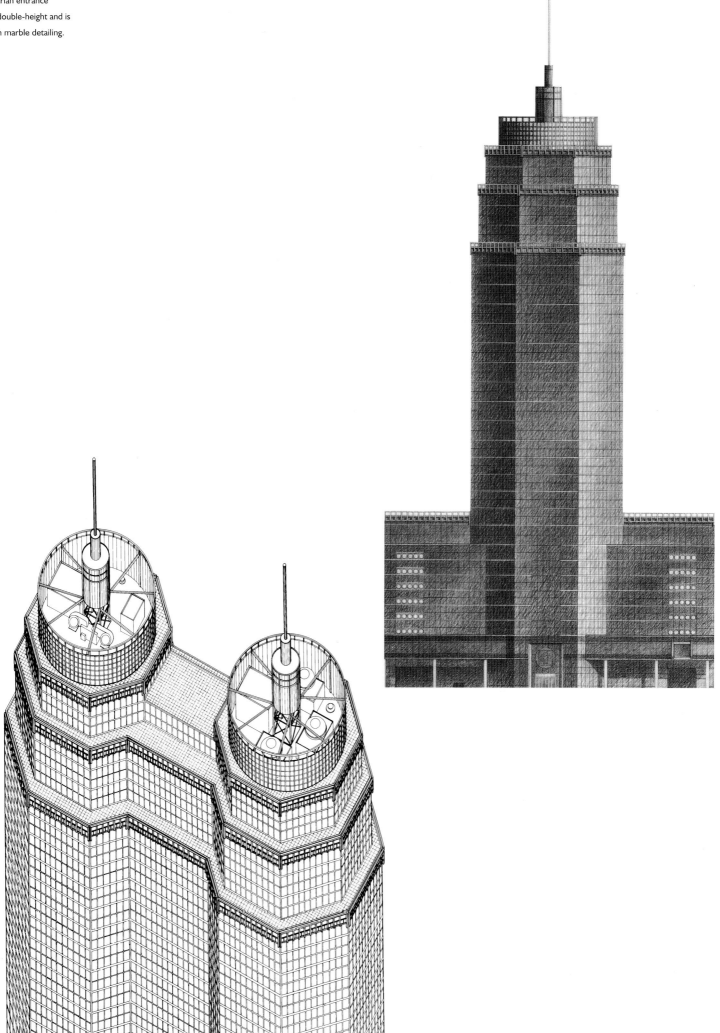

OPPOSITE:

Main pedestrian entrance
lobby rises double-height and is
finished with marble detailing.

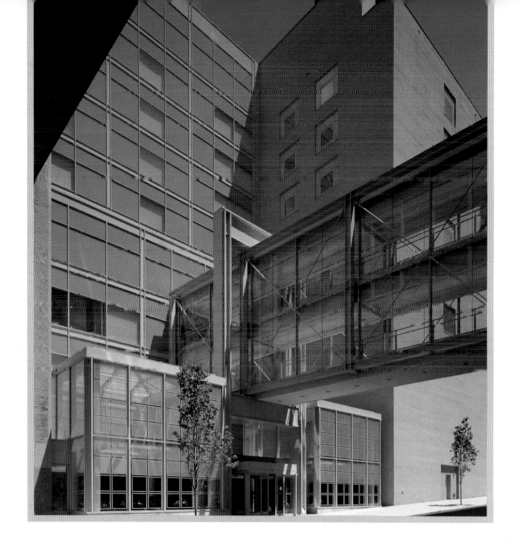

ST. LUKE'S/ROOSEVELT HOSPITAL

NEW YORK, NEW YORK

Operational efficiency is a necessity in the competitive marketplace for health care services. When two major New York City hospitals merged to form St. Luke's/Roosevelt Hospital Center, Skidmore, Owings & Merrill was hired to develop a master plan to address modernization and expansion for the united institution.

After a comprehensive analysis of the existing facilities and potential for renovation, major new medical pavilions were integrated with the most sound original building to create a cohesive medical campus. Clinical services were consolidated to eliminate redundancies, while support and processing departments were centralized to create economies of scale.

At the former St. Luke's site, the architects designed a 350,000-square-foot facility to replace three obsolete buildings. The new wing houses compact acute care, 540 patient beds, and a shared inpatient and outpatient surgical suite. A new 14-story medical tower at the Roosevelt site replaces all but one of the existing buildings. This consolidation will release a major parcel of land for independent development.

At both sites, new patient units are sized and configured to permit better use of existing medical staff. In addition, surgical suites featuring separate entrances are designed with flexibility to be used for both inpatient and ambulatory surgery.

OPPOSITE:

The new 550,000-square-foot facility houses 563 patient rooms, surgical facilities, imaging services, labor and delivery rooms, and emergency functions. The main entrance of the medical tower is marked with three large archways articulated with metal panels.

ST. VINCENT HOSPITAL WEST PAVILION

PORTLAND, OREGON

The new West Pavilion, designed by Zimmer Gunsul Frasca Partnership, is a three-story wing located adjacent to the existing St. Vincent Hospital. The primary challenge confronting the architects was the need to accommodate the functional requirements of three very large and different clinical services.

The architects organized the 206,350-square-foot facility in a stacked, multilevel configuration and designed the structure to support vertical expansion of future nursing floors atop the three-story base. In response to the existing campus architecture, the $28 million pavilion is clad in precast concrete and features deep window recesses of varying size that provide for privacy, views, and sun shading. The facility was designed with a comprehensible circulation pattern with direct access to and within each of the various departments.

The catheterization labs and surgery components of the heart services unit have common patient prep areas, staff spaces, and support and supply areas to increase efficiencies. Surgery suites are designed with built-in flexibility and can accommodate open heart and combined procedures, or catheterization treatments.

The West Pavilion also houses a new public entrance and lobby, a significantly expanded emergency and urgent care unit, and a comprehensive women's center with 32 LDRP rooms and a Level III neonatal nursery.

LEFT:
State-of-the-art nursing stations provide support for St. Vincent's emergency care unit, one of the largest on the West Coast of the United States.

RIGHT:
The heart services wing features a common patient prep area to support the catheterization lab and surgery components. Some operating rooms were designed with built-in flexibility to serve either open heart or combined surgery.

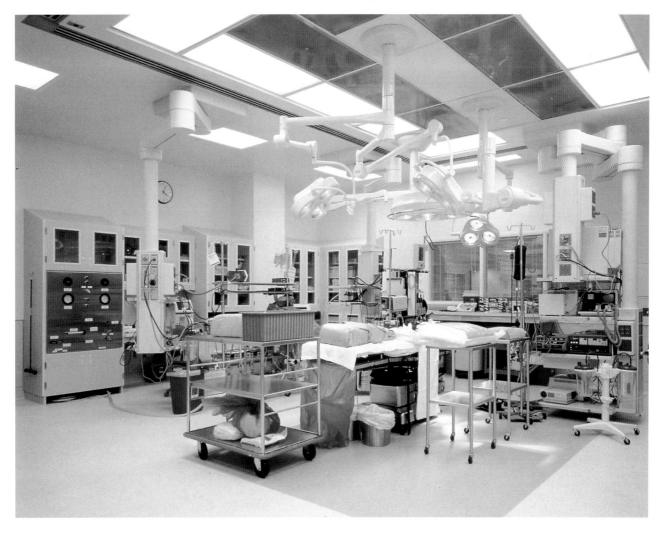

ABOVE:

From the lobby/reception area one can view a landscaped garden that features a waterfall.

OPPOSITE:

The Maternity Center is also one of the most comprehensive in the Northwest, providing obstetrical care in 32 LDRP rooms and a Level II-III neonatal nursery

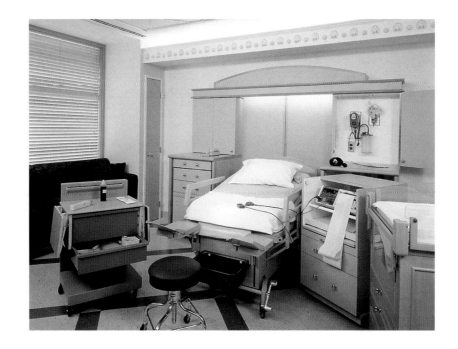

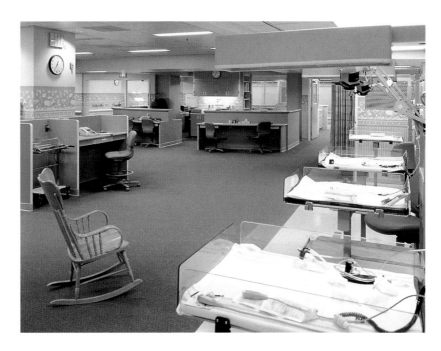

SOUTH PAVILION, ROANOKE MEMORIAL HOSPITAL

ROANOKE, VIRGINIA

MGR Architects designed the new South Pavilion at Roanoke Memorial Hospital in accordance with patient-centered care concepts. As the flag ship facility of the Carilion Health Systems, the South Pavilion is organized for optimal management and diagnostic and treatment services.

In response to tight budget constraints facing all health care providers, the South Pavilion was designed and built with a goal of cost containment. Early in the process, the architects, contractor, and the client formed a team approach for selecting materials and equipment for efficiency and durability. Floor plans were developed to increase the use of shared functions and to reduce staffing requirements.

The medical center is located on a tight urban site bordered by Mill Mountain, the Roanoke River, and city-owned property. In response to these constraints, the architects designed a curving new nine-story wing, which can accommodate future expansion of five additional floors. A curtain wall of reflective glass articulated with contrasting horizontal banding was used to lessen the apparent bulk of the new building. The 300,000-square-foot facility, which houses admissions, an emergency/trauma unit, surgery, and acute-care beds, also responds with built-in flexibility to support evolving technology.

ABOVE:

The curving facade of the South Pavilion responds to the hospital's tight urban site. The facilities house a new 30,000-square-foot emergency/trauma center, surgery, cardiac services, ICU, neuro-trauma intensive care, and progressive care units.

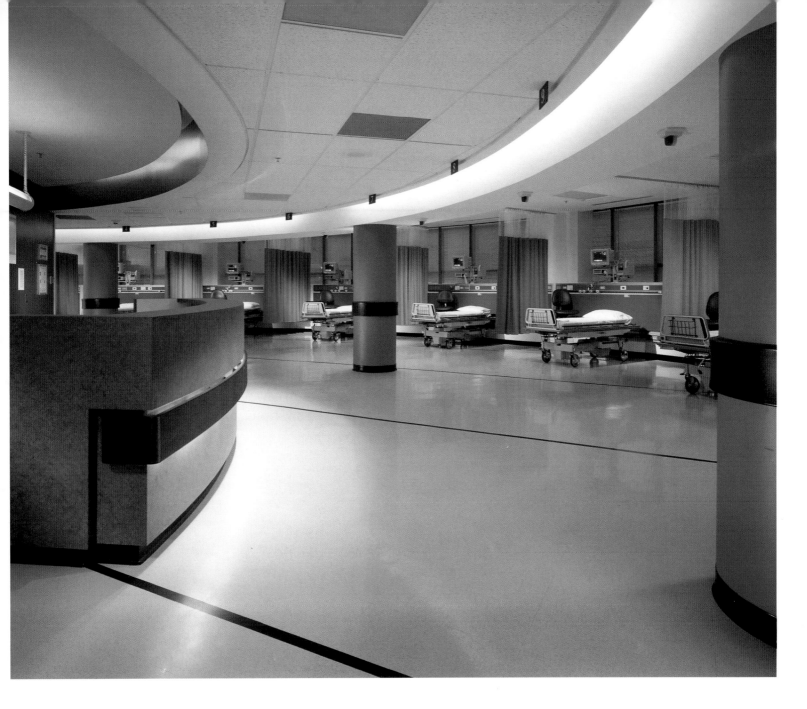

ABOVE:

The post-anesthesia care unit is arranged to take advantage of the curved floor plan. Large windows create a sense of openness.

LEFT:

Public spaces and corridors were designed for easy wayfinding. Materials, such as granite, concrete, and steel, were selected for efficiency and durability.

↑
Health Information
Management
Health Sciences Library
Medical Staff Offices

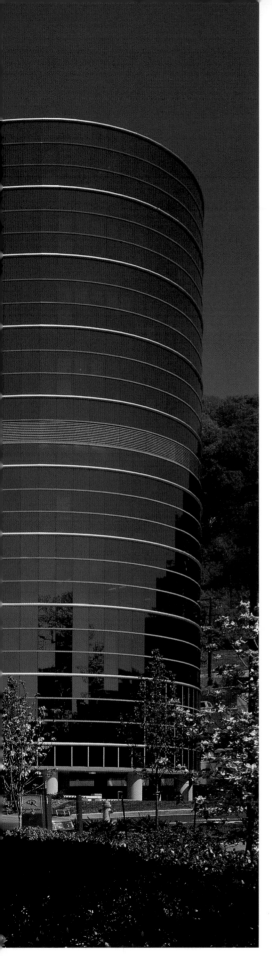

BELOW:

The critical care unit was
designed with a central nursing station surrounded by
individual patient units along
the perimeter.

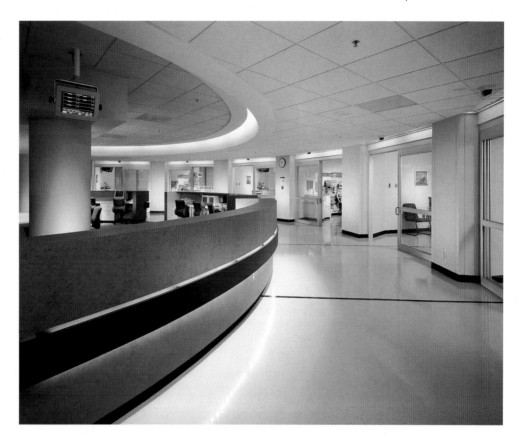

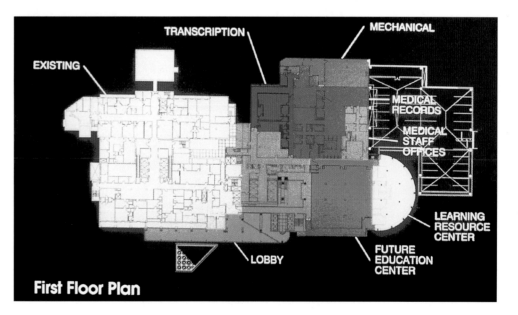

TRANSCRIPTION

MECHANICAL

EXISTING

MEDICAL
RECORDS

MEDICAL
STAFF
OFFICES

LEARNING
RESOURCE
CENTER

LOBBY

FUTURE
EDUCATION
CENTER

First Floor Plan

UNIVERSITY OF CALIFORNIA, SAN DIEGO MEDICAL CENTER

SAN DIEGO, CALIFORNIA

UCSD Medical Center's expansion program called for a new outpatient surgery center, improved vertical circulation, a new lobby, and seismic upgrade for the existing buildings. Architects Kaplan McLaughlin Diaz and Neptune-Thomas-Davis reoriented the medical center to face south and added a bold glass-and-steel entrance rotunda, shielded by three curved sunscreens fabricated of perforated steel. This new circular space, tucked between the existing hospital structures, provides a grand reception area for visitors and patients. The new vehicular approach is marked with a steel canopy and a punched granite-clad screen wall that marches out of the lobby and onto the sidewalk.

Outpatient surgery functions, including bronchoscopy, cardiology, and pulmonary, are housed in a four-story rectangular wing, situated parallel to the existing patient tower. Completing the medical complex is a new eleven-story tower, which houses four new elevators and classrooms for the medical school. Futuristic glass and stucco-clad spires crown the infill tower.

To comply with seismic codes, the architects stabilized the patient tower, built in 1962, with steel cross braces tied into the existing structural columns of the steel-framed building. The mechanical ducts on the tower's west elevation are clad in stucco embossed with a similar diagonal pattern.

OPPOSITE:

A three-tiered steel canopy
announces the vehicular drop-off
and shelters arriving patients.

ABOVE:

A new 45-foot-high glazed lobby is finished with terrazzo floors and pierced with a granite-clad screen wall that continues out to the street. Overlooking the main lobby are curved classrooms located on the second- and third-floor mezzanines.

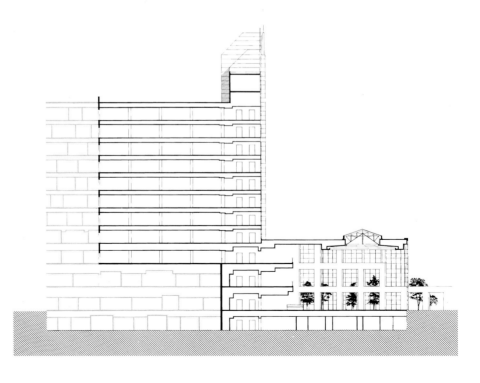

ABOVE:

The UCSD new addition fills a niche between the original 1962 rectilinear hospital and a south-facing clinic added in the 1970s. The curving glass-and-steel rotunda marks the new entrance to the expanded hospital complex.

The existing tower was renovated and upgraded to meet
earthquake standards with
new steel tie rods that span
two floors.

Cafeteria

Gift
Shop

Lobby

Pre-Admission

Admission / Bed Control

ABOVE:

The circular entrance rotunda features layered
perforated steel screens that shield the south
facing lobby. A granite-clad screen wall and
metal canopy reach out to the street.

HEALTH CENTRAL, WEST ORANGE HOSPITAL

OCOEE, FLORIDA

Designed by HKS to serve as a "one-stop shopping center" for health care services, the West Orange Health Central reorients traditional medical care with a new model for a healthier future. The complex is designed to be a source of wellness and preventive care, as well as rehabilitation from disease and injury. Accordingly, the 275,000-square-foot facility combines a 141-bed acute care hospital with physicians' suites, health services, preventive medicine, and related retail shops.

The centerpiece of the facility is a 9,000-square-foot glass atrium filled with palm trees and landscaping. The atrium hosts community events, from art shows and concerts to health fairs and medical screenings. Registration for hospital services resembles a hotel check-in desk, and most outpatient procedures are adjacent to the main reception area.

Responding to the hospital administration's request for a lively exterior, the architects broke the facility into a series of staggered components with contrasting fenestration and detailing. A bright red inverted box anchors the retail section of the complex.

Architects HKS designed the new facility with broad flexibility to accommodate technological advances and necessary expansion, as the needs of the community change and grow. One innovative component is the inclusion of a "mobile technology" port. As medical advances emerge, and before the hospital makes a permanent financial investment in new equipment, this technology port will allow trucks carrying experimental instruments to be directly attached to the hospital. The vehicle becomes part of the building as patients are wheeled directly onto and off the truck.

ABOVE:

For a dramatic image at night, the architects marked the hospital's main entrance with a bold structural canopy of steel and glass and an illuminated spire.

ABOVE
The hospital is a combination of a series of seemingly discrete structures with contrasting forms and materials that suggest the various functions.

RIGHT:
A grand stairway rises through the atrium to connect the mezzanine floors.

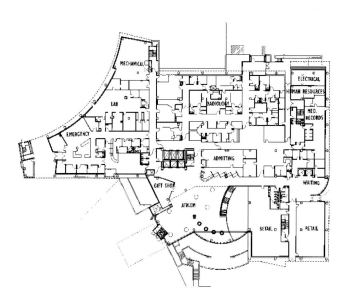

WILSON MEMORIAL REGIONAL MEDICAL CENTER, UNITED HEALTH SERVICES

BINGHAMTON, NEW YORK

The United Health Services was formed in the 1980s through the merger of three 500-bed hospitals, each serving its own local community. Decreasing population, declining acute-care census associated with the loss of major industries in the area, and cost containment pressures had severely affected the viability of the three facilities. Increasing penetration of HMOs in the market was projected, and the reimbursement system was slated for change.

Kaplan McLaughlin Diaz was hired to develop a master plan for the consolidated medical institutions, which called for a clearly differentiated mission for each facility and a new 87,000-square-foot diagnostic, treatment, and outpatient center at the Wilson campus. In anticipation of

varying patient volumes, the architects designed departments to "telescope," or provide for the efficient operation of a unit at full census or accommodate reduced staffing when the patient count decreases.

To give the new outpatient center a strong visual presence, the architects created a patterned brick exterior enlivened with precast accents and ornate window treatments. The architects chose interior finishes to reinforce the facility's noninstitutional image, including maple floors and railings, brick walls, and custom built-in furnishings. An art program featuring paintings and collages by neighborhood children strengthens the hospital's ties to the community.

Photo: © Jeff Goldberg/Esto

LEFT:

Located on a dense site, the new facility was sited to create little garden pockets.

ABOVE:

The architects clad the facility with an ornamental brick pattern enlivened with precast window details to create a strong image that conveys quality and stability without extravagance.

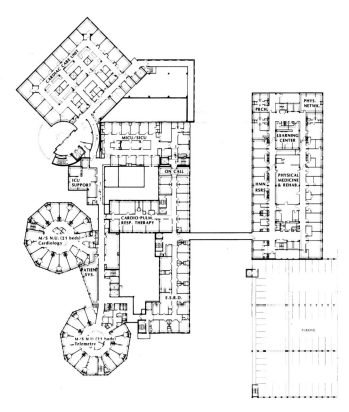

LEFT:

The exterior's brick, window details, and ornamentation were intended to recall architectural traditions of the community.

ABOVE:

Clear and convenient access and circulation were achieved through separate entries for patients and staff and comprehensible pathways for outpatient services.

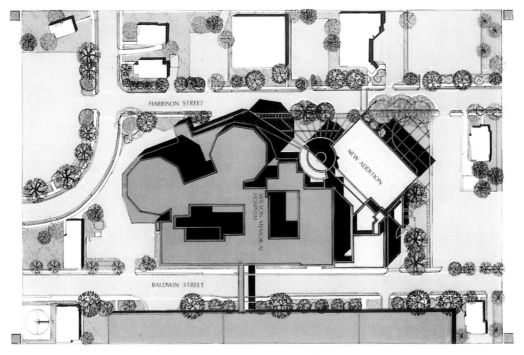

HARRISON STREET

WILSON MEMORIAL HOSPITAL

NEW ADDITION

BALDWIN STREET

SITE PLAN

ACADIA HOSPITAL

BANGOR, MAINE

Guided by the metaphor of vernacular New England architecture of the farmhouse, barn, and field, Cannon Architects organized this private, nonprofit psychiatric hospital into a campus arrangement with domestically scaled buildings. The 126,000-square-foot facility, which accommodates both inpatient care and a comprehensive day program, is clad in painted clapboard and wood shingles.

The main building of the compound—the farmhouse—accommodates inpatient functions including admissions, dining area, and crisis intervention. This central communal space allows for ease of access and control for staff, while the rooms open up with curved glass walls to create an open feeling for patients.

This structure also houses a 22-bed chemical dependency unit, a 24-bed adult wing, a 24-bed older adult unit, a 16-bed adolescent section, and a 10-bed children's wing. Patient rooms are organized around back-to-back nursing stations so that a unit can be expanded or reduced depending on census, without compromising the separation of the populations.

An existing osteopathic facility on the grounds was renovated with a new roof and wood shingle cladding to mirror the design of the new hospital. The main entrance of the complex is housed in a barnlike structure, designed as a loft space to house the public lobby and reception area. In profile beyond the portico and entrance building is a gymnasium.

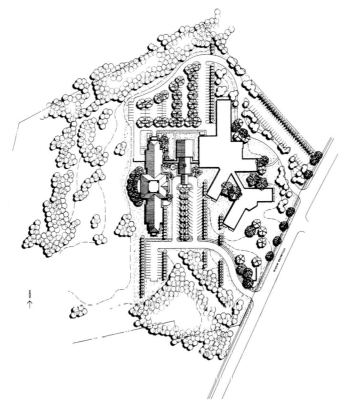

ABOVE:

A welcoming new entrance features a gabled portico. An enclosed wood and glass loggia, the primary circulation corridor, links all three buildings.

ABOVE:

Cannon designed the Acadia Hospital to blend with the surrounding residential neighborhood.

LEFT:

An outdoor patio is used for meetings, informal gatherings, and dining in nice weather.

RIGHT:

Patient rooms are organized around a centralized nursing station. Common areas have a residential organization and are traditionally furnished to create a reassuring environment.

LAUREL RIDGE PSYCHIATRIC HOSPITAL

SAN ANTONIO, TEXAS

The Laurel Ridge Psychiatric Hospital is organized around a village square and designed as an integrated community. Dallas architects HKS designed the facility for flexible treatment programs to provide a continuum of psychiatric care for children, adolescents, and adults. The complex includes a 160-bed freestanding inpatient hospital and a comprehensive outpatient clinic that supports after care and day and evening treatment programs.

The architects designed the campus to accommodate the varied populations and functions and to provide a gradual transition from public to private spaces. The patient living areas are designed as residential neighborhoods, clustered around landscaped courtyards and a central education building. In response to the region's tradition of Spanish Colonial architecture, the architects used warm natural stucco, red tile roofs, and arcades. The various buildings of the complex are connected by arched colonnades, and accent bands of royal blue tiles make the exterior walls more lively. At the axis point of private and public circulation stands a 670-foot-tall bell tower, a focal point from within the complex and beyond.

Throughout the interiors, the architects repeated traditional detailing with glue-lam beams and wood ceilings. Cupolas are used to allow clerestory light into central public spaces.

ABOVE:

At night the prominent bell tower provides a beacon at an entrance to the Laurel Ridge campus.

OPPOSITE:

Arched colonnades provide sheltered circulation between the various buildings of the campus facility.

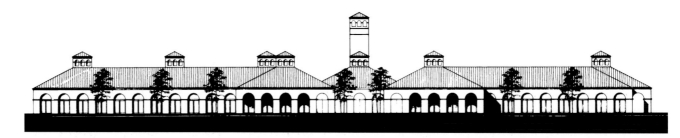

ABOVE:

Reflecting the indigenous architecture of the region, small-scale buildings of stucco with red-tiled roofs are clustered around landscaped courtyards to create a nurturing environment.

LEFT:

Meandering pathways lead
through the landscaped
grounds of the Laurel
Ridge facility.

LEFT:

Colorful geometric pavers animate the
walkways that connect the clustered
buildings of the campus.

ABOVE:

In response to the rich design traditions
of San Antonio, HKS chose a Spanish-
style architecture for the Laurel Ridge
campus, accentuated by red tile roofs,
arches, colonnades, and a bell tower.

JOHN GEORGE PSYCHIATRIC PAVILION
ALAMEDA COUNTY DEPT. OF HEALTH SERVICES

SAN LEANDRO, CALIFORNIA

The concept of creating special surroundings for a group of people sharing a common affliction is not new. Changing attitudes toward society's view of individuals in need of psychiatric services have resulted in reforms that have greatly improved the physical environment of mental health facilities. The Ratcliff Architects' design of the John George Psychiatric Pavilion reflects this heightened sensitivity to the emotional problems of clients and to the concerns of the professional staff who work at the facility. The planning and design focused on a noninstitutional atmosphere, intended to encourage social interaction among patients and between staff and patients and to create a state-of-the-art hospital.

Located on a prominent hilltop site, the John George Pavilion is reminiscent of an Italian hill town. The architects clustered the five buildings of the complex around a central village green. A symbolic clock tower marks the main entrance to the campus, while the administration building serves as the town center, housing regular day activities, such as occupational and recreational therapy. Under a curved arcade within the village green, the 80 residents are grouped into neighborhoods, with bedrooms opening onto intimately scaled living and dining areas. Each residential wing includes a landscaped courtyard.

All hospitals are under intense pressure to control operating cost while providing first-rate care. Accordingly, the architects incorporated flexibility and cost-effectiveness into their design through the use of "swing beds." These allow for adjusting the size of units to accommodate varying numbers of clients of different ages and acuity levels as patient census levels change. Shared support staff areas also help to combine staff functions and minimize duplication of services.

OPPOSITE:
Structural frames and carpeted seating areas subdivide the central space into more intimate areas.

LEFT:
The clock tower marks the main public approach up the hillside to the facility.

ABOVE:

A curved arcade fronts the landscaped courtyard. Individual front doors announce the entrance to each of the three living units.

RIGHT AND OPPOSITE:

The cluster arrangement provides for a series of outdoor community spaces, including both active and quiet areas.

CHILDREN'S HOSPITAL AND HEALTH CENTER

SAN DIEGO, CALIFORNIA

A new 187,000-square-foot patient wing at Children's Hospital, designed by NBBJ, alleviates severe crowding at the 40-year-old medical institution. But, more importantly, this new wing affords not only the space but the opportunity to practice a new kind of medicine, one that is sensitive to what scares children and what helps them recover, and one that involves the entire family in the healing process.

Situated between two busy north-south freeways, Children's Hospital looks like a fantasy castle atop a mesa perch, with its red roofs, a 60-foot-tall clock tower, lively articulated facades, and playful detailing. The ground floor is visually organized with gray concrete block accented with horizontal bands of red and white scaled to the height of children. As well, familiar residential forms and ornaments provide a psychological comfort for children upon their arrival.

Visitors enter through the base of the clock tower to a square main lobby, which doubles as a reception area and waiting room for families of children being treated. A pair of admission desks anchors the two corners of the clock tower. On the second floor, thirty-bed nursing sections become neighborhoods, with ten patient rooms clustered around a nursing station designed to recall images of home. This compact design gives nurses more immediate access to each child. Above all, NBBJ's design balances the serious business of caring for ailing children with a spirit of playfulness and fun.

OPPOSITE:

First-floor lobby features a circular
reception desk finished in stainless
steel and plastic laminate, and
designed to resemble a toy drum.

ABOVE:

The first-floor restaurant is
marked with a whimsical neon
sign. Colorful chairs double as
recycling bins.

OPPOSITE:

A fiber-optic constellation of twinkling lights animate the ceiling above the nursing station.

ABOVE:

The Children's Hospital was divided into a series of pavilions. The architects inserted a second-floor play court within a curving wall with punched windows.

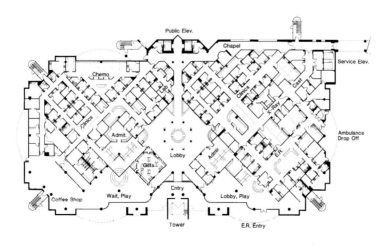

FIRST FLOOR

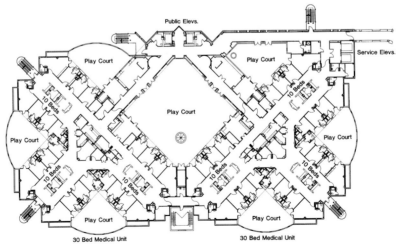

SECOND FLOOR

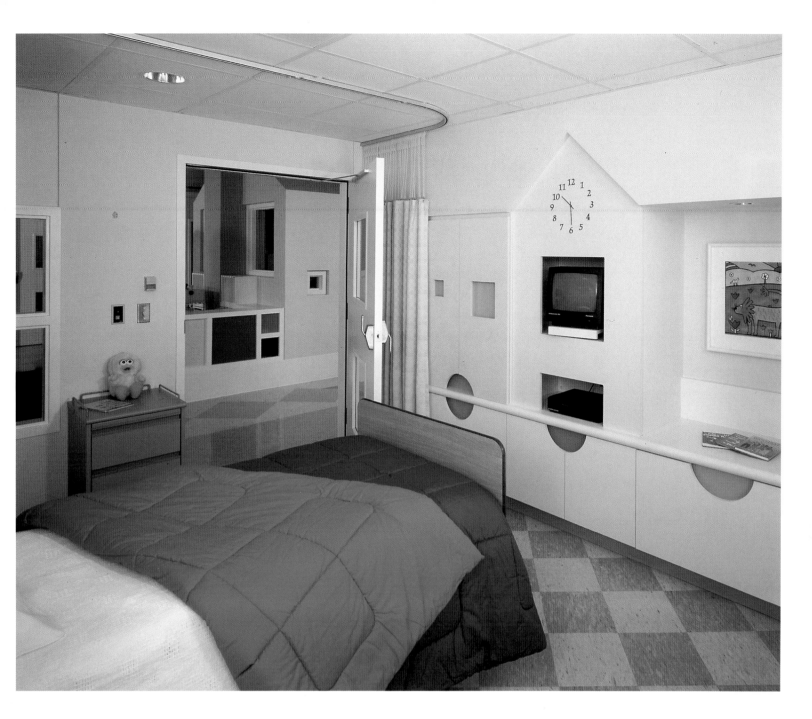

OPPOSITE:

The play area on the patient wing features recessed, colorful circular seating and provides space for organized and individual recreational activities.

ABOVE:

Individual patient rooms were designed with built-in custom fixtures and playful details to evoke images of home.

Photo: © Peter Aaron/Esto

CHILDREN'S HOSPITAL AT YALE NEW HAVEN HOSPITAL

NEW HAVEN, CONNECTICUT

The new Children's Hospital at Yale New Haven Hospital represents a trend toward reducing the scale and anonymity of large medical centers by targeting centers of excellence within an institution and creating smaller, more focused entities. Adjacent to the main hospital, the new 450,000-square-foot pediatrics facility, designed by Boston architects Shepley Bulfinch Richardson and Abbott, is integrated within the medical campus to increase the use of common support functions and diagnostic services while providing the young patients with a less threatening institutional environment.

The Children's Hospital is the first phase of a long-term master plan for the entire Yale New Haven complex, which is scheduled to be reorganized as four patient care pavilions centered around a central atrium. To create a visual link with the brick and tile of the existing buildings, the architects clad the exterior of the new, 11-story children's tower with a combination of smooth and aggregate precast concrete panels. Conforming to the master plan, a new, 45-foot-high, skylit atrium directly links the three existing medical buildings by providing a central gathering and eating space for visitors, patients, and staff.

Patient rooms in the children's tower are arranged in a clustered neighborhood concept with between eight and ten private rooms positioned in cloverleaf fashion around a central nursing station. This configuration defies the institutional stereotype of endless corridors by creating a series of connected large spaces. No bed is further than 100 feet from a nursing station, and the clusters are designed for easy conversion to step-down or ICU units in the future.

OPPOSITE:

The Children's Hospital entry is a drive-through; centered within this space is an up-lit octagonal garden pavilion, with seating and a commemorative bronze statue of a young girl in a carefree pose.

ABOVE:

The new Children's Tower is a distinct, recognizable new entity within the Yale New Haven Hospital Complex.

LEFT:

Four patient care wings center on an interior skylit atrium, which features a lively fountain, granite benches, and intimate seating areas.

ABOVE:

Activity rooms and patient
lounges were designed to alleviate some of the stress and
anxiety typically associated
with large-scale urban medical
centers. Colorful custom furnishings enliven these community spaces.

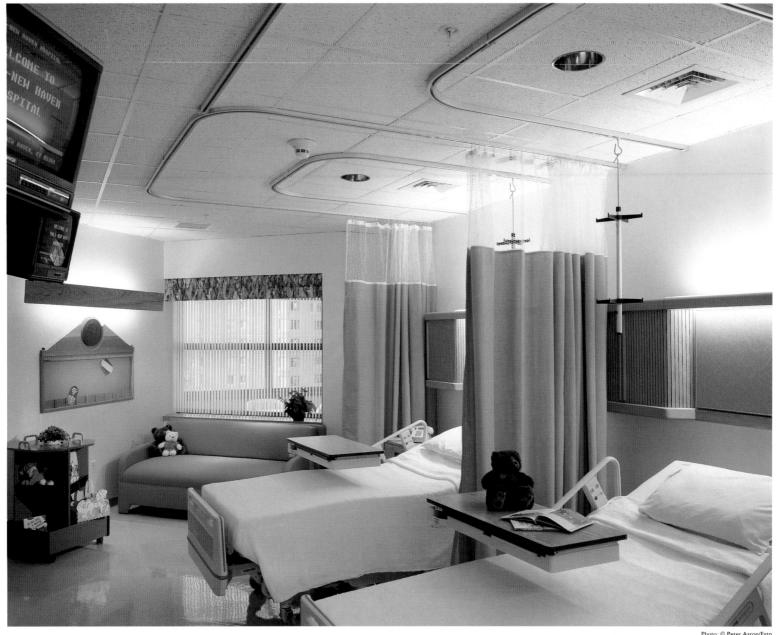

ABOVE:

Generous semiprivate patient rooms feature furniture and built-in fixtures scaled to meet the needs of young patients.

RIGHT:

The new Children's Tower also houses a comprehensive and expanded maternity center with pleasant LDR suites.

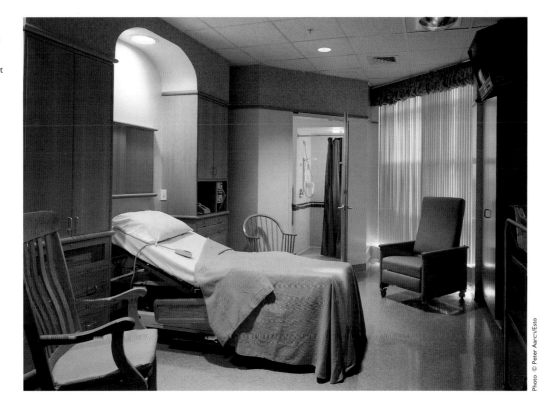

THE HOSPITAL FOR SICK CHILDREN

TORONTO, ONTARIO

Expanding a medical center located in a tight urban location is one of the greatest challenges facing health care architects. For the Hospital for Sick Children in Toronto, Zeidler Roberts Partnership demolished an existing parking garage and two obsolete buildings to free up space for 1.2 million square feet of new construction.

Pediatric patient floors consist of 96 inpatient rooms organized in four "pods," each with a central nursing station and a corner play area that overlooks the central atrium. The four pods are arranged to support staff adjacencies and efficient delivery of medical services. To achieve an environment that best responds to the emotional needs of

a sick child, the architects designed single patient rooms, each equipped with a private bathroom and sofa bed so that a parent may spend the night with the child.

To impart clarity and order within this massive new medical complex, the architects organized functions around a central atrium that rises eight stories high. A new entrance facing east encourages pedestrian traffic from the city and is connected with the atrium by an interior "Main Street." This interior organization accommodates future expansion. The hospital's next phase, now underway, provides for the conversion of existing buildings within the complex to house ambulatory care and research.

OPPOSITE:

At night the new glazed atrium of the Hospital for Sick Children is illuminated and stands in contrast with the brick facades of the hospital complex.

148 **PEDIATRIC FACILITIES**

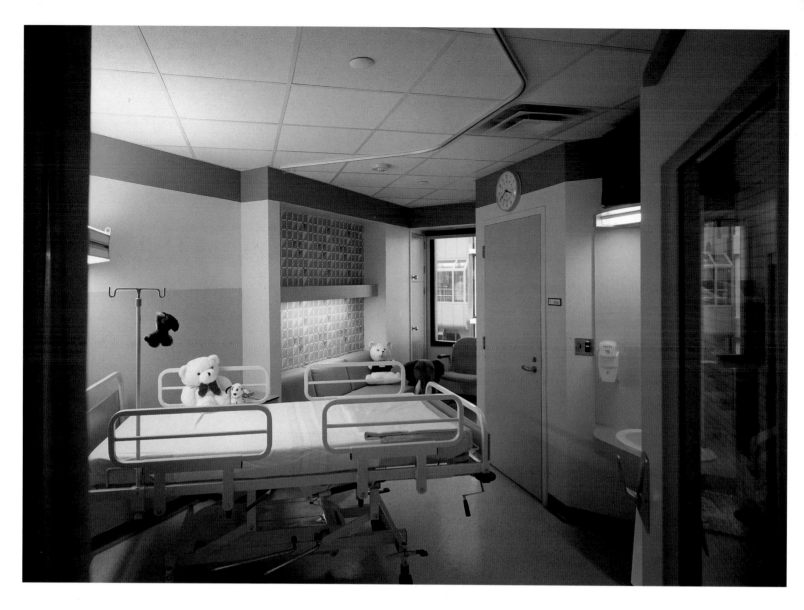

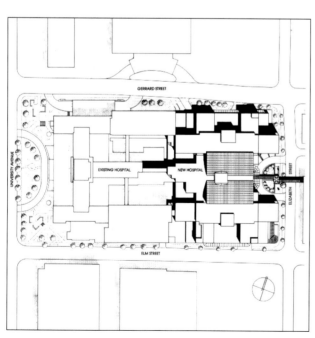

SITE PLAN

LEFT:

Patient rooms are equipped with private baths and a sofa bed so a parent may spend the night with the child.

RIGHT:

A new glass and steel pedestrian bridge provides an important linkage between the atrium and existing structures.

BELOW:

Glass-enclosed stairwells contribute to the open and airy atmosphere in the central atrium.

The Atrium
The Hospital for Sick Children
170 Elizabeth Street
Parking   Emergency

WASHINGTON HOSPITAL FOR SICK CHILDREN

WASHINGTON, D.C.

A long-term convalescent facility that treats infants and children in transition between acute care and the home, the Hospital for Sick Children recently added a new patient wing and administration and conference center, designed by Weinstein Associates Architects and Herbert Cohen & Associates. The typical stay is 110 days, and up to 96 percent of the patients are cared for through Medicare.

The original hospital, built in 1928 as a children's "country home," is an eclectic collage of Norman and English cottage–revival architecture. In deference to the historic structure, the architects clad the new two-story wings with an ornamental brick pattern in three colors, and reduced the apparent mass of the two-story structure with

a series of carefully placed niches and bays. The smooth exterior walls are enriched with reinterpreted English cottage detailing, such as quoining, incised arches, and brick nogging.

Inside the new patient wing, designed in association with the Washington office of RTKL, the focus is on responding to the unique needs of the children who reside there. The facility incorporates abundant natural light, stylized floor patterns, warm textures, and wooden handrails to create a friendly, homelike environment. Recreational areas, segregated from clinical functions, provide safe havens where shots and unpleasant procedures are never administered.

OPPOSITE:

The new wing of the Hospital for
Sick Children with its intricate
pattern of bricks was designed
to complement the existing 1929
Norman-style buildings.

ABOVE:

The mass of the new, two-story
wing is broken with carefully
placed niches and bays.

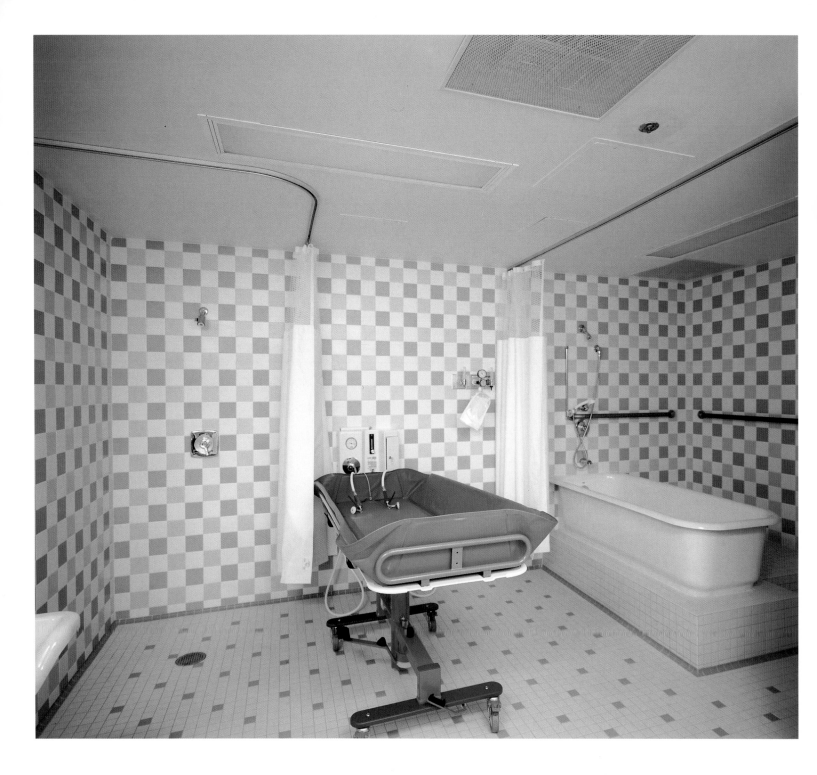

ABOVE:

Floor and wall tiles are used to create stylized patterns while providing tough and easy-to-maintain surfaces.

LEFT:

Nursing stations are centrally located. Flat floors with smooth high-traction surfaces make it easy to maneuver special wheelchairs.

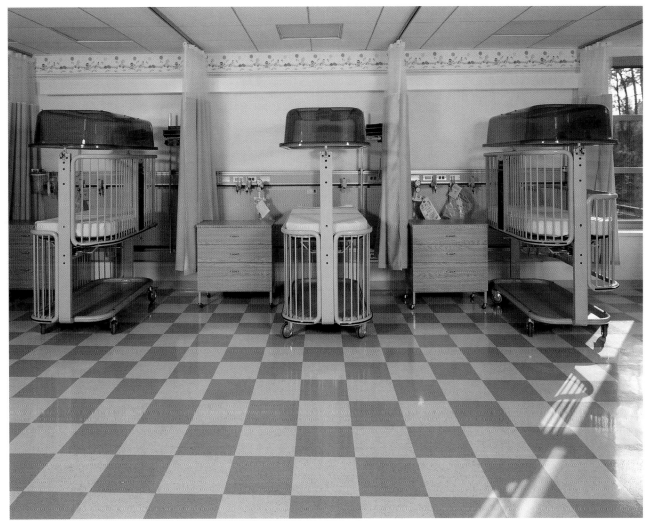

LEFT:

The interiors reflect the special requirements of the clients of the hospital. With large windows, the nursery was designed as a light and airy space and accommodates multiple cribs.

LEFT AND BELOW:
The architects decorated the
hospital in an engaging tricolor
pattern of bricks and tucked a
stair tower behind a curving
facade that appears to unfurl
from the mass of the structure.

KIRK SCHARFENBERG HOUSE
FOR CHILDREN WITH AIDS

MATTAPAN, MASSACHUSETTS

A prototype for a pediatric AIDS program, the Kirk Scharfenberg House was designed by Buck, Smith & McAvoy as a comprehensive respite program to provide residential and day-care for HIV-infected children.

The facility is located on the campuslike grounds of the Mattapan Chronic Disease Hospital and is adjacent to the director's house, built at the turn of the century. Project architect Julia Smith designed the 9,000-square-foot facility as a rambling, one-story, Victorian-style house with a modified L-shaped floor plan. This configuration allows for a variety of setbacks, verandas, and a sweeping gabled roof that reduces the scale of the building and gives the institution a decidedly residential character.

The building is sited with public activities facing the main street and served by a front access with a vehicular drop-off. A rear driveway leads to a simple entry porch which accommodates deliveries, staff, and emergency vehicles. The day-care area is separated from the overnight-care area by a spine of administrative offices and support functions.

Representing a truly collaborative community effort, a group of 25 local designers called the Boston Interior Design Community, coordinated a fundraising drive and volunteered their services in designing the facility and furnishing the rooms.

OPPOSITE:

Hats, coats, and boots drape a playful painted landscape in the vestibule of the respite home.

LEFT:

The architects gave the facility a decidedly residential feel by incorporating Victorian detailing, gazebo porches, and a gabled roof.

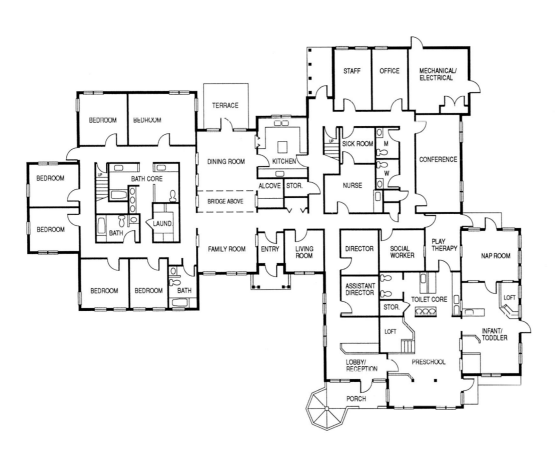

SHRINERS HOSPITAL FOR CRIPPLED CHILDREN

MINNEAPOLIS, MINNESOTA

Reflecting the trend toward family-centered care, the Shriners Hospital for Crippled Children, designed by Odell Associates, responds to a child's affliction while providing a range of family unit support services to complement the care of the young patient.

The 120,000-square-foot, two-story structure is organized with outpatient services on the first level and inpatient care on the second. To create a friendly exterior facade, the architects crowned the building with a series of gabled roofs and enlivened the red brick walls with green mullions, granite accents, and horizontal limestone bandings.

Inside, every attempt was made to deinstitutionalize the facility. Large skylit atrium spaces integrate the main lobby with outpatient receiving areas. Wood is used for bases, handrails, and ceilings to add textural warmth, and gently curving nurses' stations create a homelike atmosphere. Inpatient rooms feature a residential scale with stylized door surrounds in various color schemes. The facility also houses a separate parents' pavilion with six hotel rooms connected by an elevated, enclosed corridor to the inpatient wing. This helps encourage parents to accompany children into the pre-op holding and recovery rooms.

ABOVE:

A double-height reception area features floor-to-ceiling windows and a prominent elevator. Lush greenery and warm wood tones add to the homey atmosphere.

To reduce the apparent
mass of the hospital, Odell
Associates broke the facility
into a series of smaller wings
crowned with peaked roofs
and clad in brick with colorful
accents.

RAIL ROAD

EAST RIVER TERRACE

CECIL STREET

TERRACE LANDSCAPING

AREAWAY

WALKWAY

SENTRY AREA

PAVILION

LANDSCAPED TERRACES

COOLING TOWERS

PARKING GARAGE

SIGN

PROPERTY LINE

EXISTING WOODED AREA

EAST RIVER ROAD

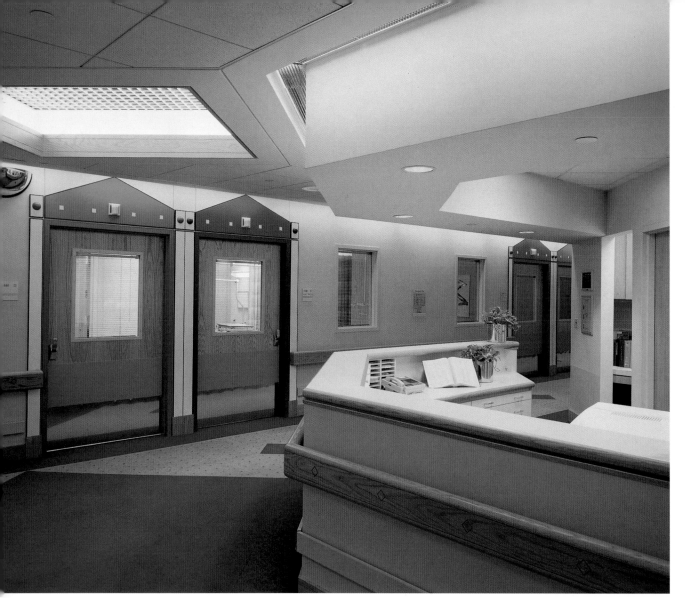

LEFT:

Patient rooms are identified with residentially stylized door surrounds in bold, primary color schemes.

OPPOSITE:

A large skylit atrium serves as the lobby and outpatient receiving areas on the first floor. Magenta chairs and a colorfully painted playhouse lend a friendly, inviting feeling to the space.

32-E

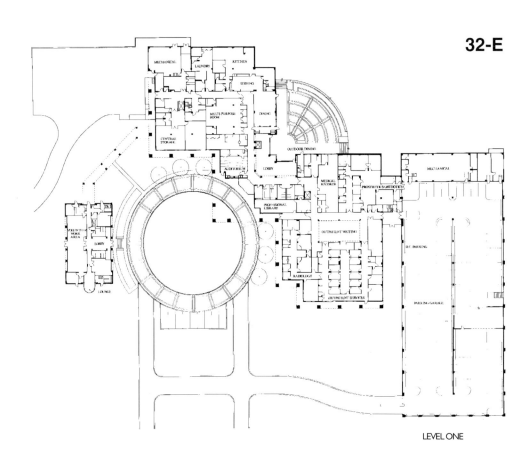

LEVEL ONE

REHABCENTRE, SOUTH FULTON MEDICAL CENTER

EAST POINT, GEORGIA

The new Rehabcentre at South Fulton Medical Center was designed by Nix Mann and Associates to reflect the institution's philosophy that the environment should support and further patients' treatment whenever possible. The 14,600-square-foot unit was organized to encourage a range of healing techniques by allowing patients more independence and breaking down the traditional hierarchy of an institutional setting. The architects located all staff, from director to therapists, within the immediate Rehabcentre environment. All treatment areas and administrative spaces are easily accessible by every patient and family member.

The architects used bright colors, warm textures in wood paneling, and patterned carpeting to infuse the center with a familiar and residential feel. Nurse's stations were made into approachable meeting places, and focal points, including an aquarium and reading nook, to draw patients along the corridors and encourage free movement.

Patient rooms are designed to give individuals the most control over their environment. Draperies allow the patient to control the amount of natural light, and lamps are activated with an easy-touch base. Built-in cabinets in the patient rooms screen technical equipment and provide shelter for sleeping patients.

OPPOSITE:

The "activities for daily living" suite is a self-contained apartment where patients and their families practice adjusting to life outside the institutional environment.

ABOVE:

The architects designed the nursing station as an approachable "meeting place" that encourages patients to interact with medical staff.

RIGHT:

Patient rooms feature colorful walls, built-in furnishings, and adjustable mirrors.

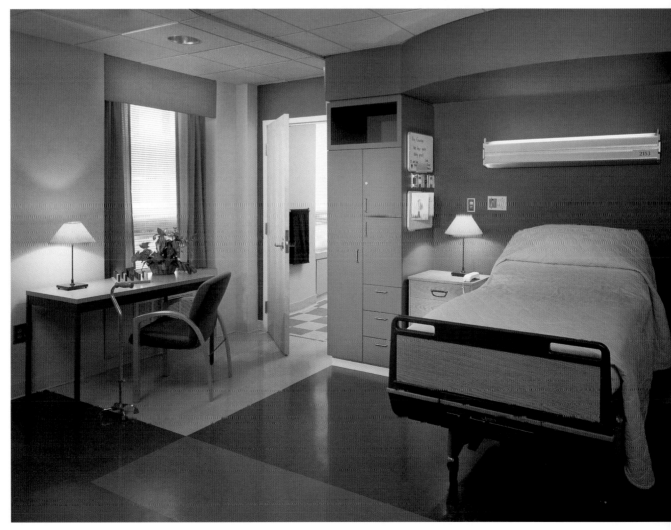

SHENANDOAH REGIONAL CAMPUS
LEARNING SERVICES CORPORATION

MANASSAS, VIRGINIA

The Shenandoah Regional Campus, designed by Atlanta architects Richard Rauh & Associates, provides transient residential convalescent care and therapy for victims of traumatic head injuries. The concept and need for such a facility is a relatively recent phenomena. Before the advent of high-technology emergency medical care, many of the clients at Shenandoah would not have survived their initial injuries.

Located on the site of an abandoned nineteenth-century estate, the Shenandoah campus is a six-building complex that includes both renovated and new buildings. The entire campus is wheelchair accessible, but the facility does not resemble a hospital environment that cushions its occupants. Many patients are cognitively as well as physi-

cally compromised, so a major part of their treatment is relearning how to function in traditional settings and deal with physical barriers.

Treatment and therapy functions are deliberately segregated from the living areas. Shenandoah's patient bedrooms are dispersed into three individual houses to lessen their bulk and to blend with the scale of the residential neighborhood. The three residences are designed to meet the varying level of support required by the clients, but the differences are very subtle to avoid stigmatizing the occupants. The architects arranged the new buildings around a central courtyard, with backyards for recreational activities and a formal front lawn facing the street.

OPPOSITE:

At night, the living room of the Dogwood House radiates warmth. Rauh placed a fireplace on direct axis with the front door of the building.

Photo: © Peter Mauss/Esto

LEFT:
The architect linked the "teaching barn" to existing structures with a pergola of concrete piers and log trellis.

BELOW:
A new two-story "teaching barn" stands beside two renovated farm buildings.

Photo: © Peter Mauss/Esto

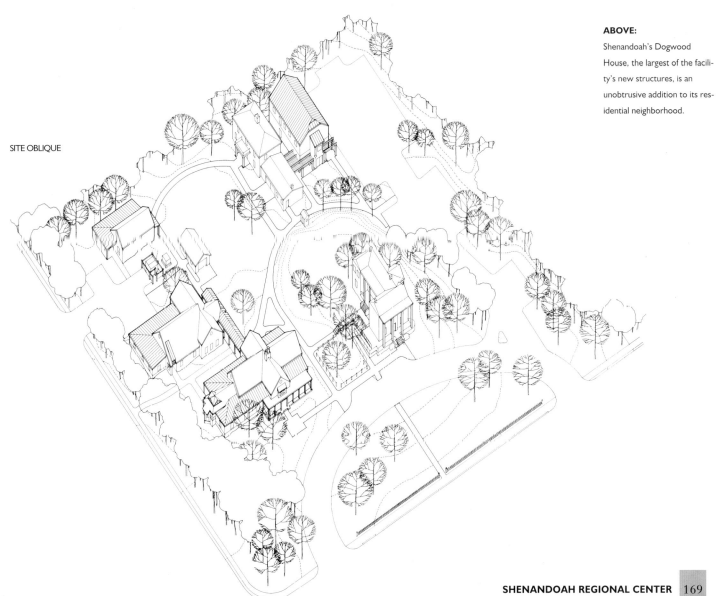

SITE OBLIQUE

ABOVE:

Shenandoah's Dogwood House, the largest of the facility's new structures, is an unobtrusive addition to its residential neighborhood.

Photo: © Peter Mauss/Esto

Photo: © Peter Mauss/Esto

LEFT:
Interiors of the residences, like the cozy library, respond to the special needs of the users without sacrificing comfort and familiarity.

ABOVE:
The dining area resembles an informal family dining room rather than an institutional cafeteria.

Photo: © Peter Mauss/Esto

Photo: © Peter Mauss/Esto

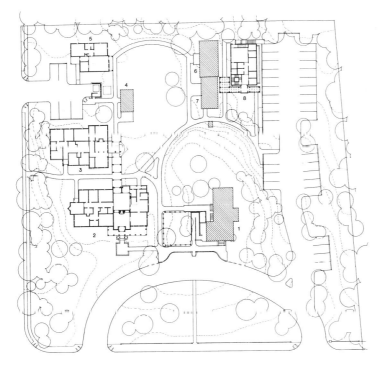

ORCHARD PAVILION, MATERNAL AND CHILD HEALTH CENTER AT EL CAMINO HOSPITAL

MOUNTAIN VIEW, CALIFORNIA

One of the biggest challenges facing health care architects is the need to plan for flexibility and to accommodate system changes. Architects Lee Burkhart Liu successfully met this goal in designing El Camino Hospital's new Orchard Pavilion. The original program started out as a 209,000-square-foot maternal and child health center with medical offices. Midway through construction, the architects were asked to incorporate a Level III neonatal intensive care unit within the facility, which required adding 10,000 square feet to the original scheme.

The Orchard Pavilion is a major component of the hospital's wellness campus, but the facility was designed as a freestanding building with its own entrance and street identity. The Pavilion's interior arrangement encourages staff efficiency and reinforces referral patterns.

The incorporation of back-to-back nursing stations allows staff to serve the postpartum units as well as adjacent pediatric rooms. During the day each four-room cluster has a satellite nursing alcove, while at night the nursing functions are consolidated at a single central station. To meet fluctuations in patient census, the architects designed swing beds and placed support functions to allow interdepartmental access.

OPPOSITE:

An illuminated canopy and graphics announce the entrance of the new freestanding Orchard Pavilion in this view at dusk.

LEFT:

Inside the Orchard Pavilion, the architects used maple hand railings and fabric-covered built-in seating nooks along curving windows.

BELOW:

Patient rooms are clustered in groups of four around a central, skylit nursing station for optimal staffing and maximum utilization of space.

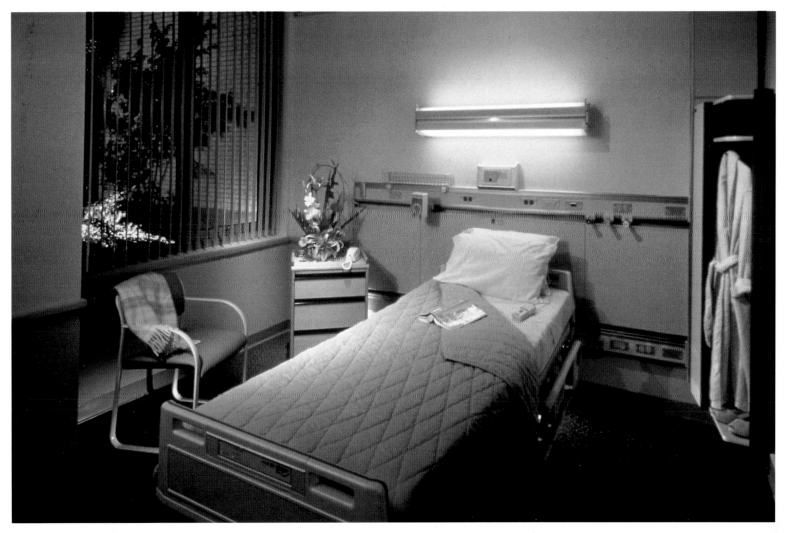

ABOVE:

The use of varied geometric
forms, as seen here in the
pitched roof and bay window,
minimize the institutional
image of the facility.

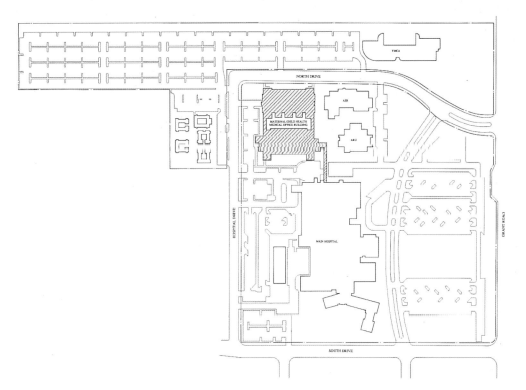

ABOVE:

The architects clad the building in three complementary colors of brick, alternated the height of the roof lines, and varied the window patterns to reduce the apparent mass of the building.

WOMEN'S CENTER, POMONA VALLEY HOSPITAL AND MEDICAL CENTER

POMONA, CALIFORNIA

The Women's Center, designed by NBBJ, is the first phase of a five-phase master plan that establishes the architectural framework for future growth and replacement of the existing Pomona Valley Hospital.

Responsive to their diverse clientele, the hospital trustees challenged NBBJ to design a facility that would be accessible and understandable to people of all backgrounds. Accordingly, the architects organized the 190,000-square-foot building with a straightforward circulation pattern. Each medical department has similar architectural details and easy-to-understand graphics. Main public circulation paths are typically located along perimeter walls, further enhancing orientation and providing natural light.

Although the Women's Center provides a full range of health care services and programs for women, the archi-

tects' desire was to create a noninstitutional image. Rather than treating the labor/delivery/recovery/postpartum, or LDRP, as a single room, the architects created a suite comprised of the main birthing room and a smaller inglenook for family gatherings. This allows family members to use the room without disturbing the mother. This LDRP suite configuration actually influenced the overall plan of the building: the need for windows in the suites created a double courtyard plan with support services in between. The four corners of the structure were opened up to emit daylight and provide easily accessible outdoor space on the second and third floors.

The color and material palette for the building consists of a red sandstone base with warm, creamy colored precast concrete panels above. The windows feature large precast surrounds coated with a green patina finish with white accents.

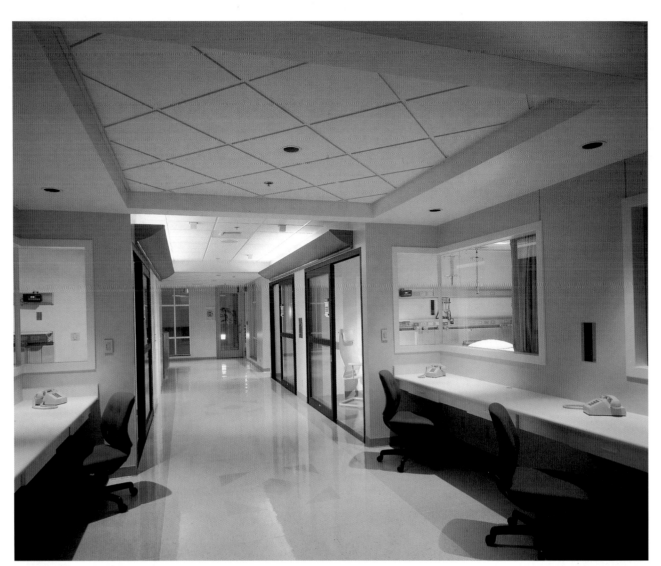

LEFT:

Nursing substations are located in the corners of the buildings and provide for separate staff and service circulation from public areas.

RIGHT:

Corridors feature vaulted ceilings and large windows.

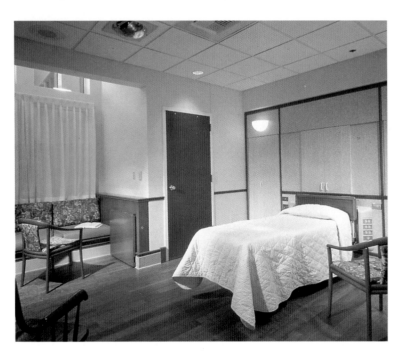

ABOVE:

Each LDRP suite contains a small inglenook for family gatherings to celebrate the birth. Beneath the window is a sofa that converts to a bed.

ABOVE:

In the main reception area, sandstone walls echo the exterior's red sandstone base.

OPPOSITE:
An evening view from an
open air lounge.

RIGHT:
NBBJ chose a red sandstone
base with cream-colored precast concrete panels above.
The windows feature large
precast surrounds coated with
a green patina finish with
white accents.

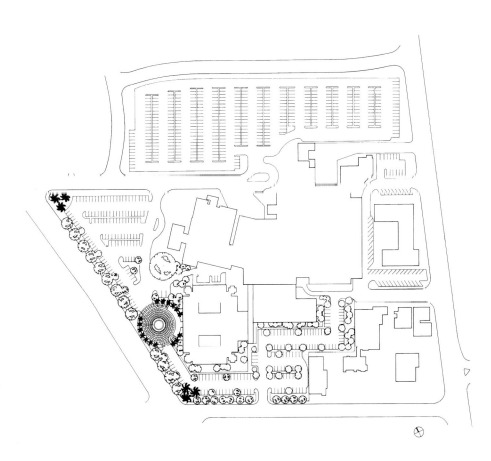

WOMEN'S PAVILION, GWINNETT MEDICAL CENTER

LAWRENCEVILLE, GEORGIA

Focusing on total health care for women with an emphasis on education, the Women's Pavilion is a freestanding facility on the grounds of the Gwinnett Medical Center. Atlanta architects Nix Mann and Associates designed this 58,000-square-foot facility to create a nonthreatening atmosphere for patients who, by and large, are not sick. To break up the apparent bulk of the center, the architects designed a highly sculptural building, comprised of plans and volumes assembled in a layered configuration. Exterior facades are enlivened with alternating glass walls and patterned brick surfaces to create a series of solids and voids. Outside stairways, punched windows, and glass block partitions further reduce the building's scale.

The facility is organized into two levels. Mothers entering from the patient drop-off or emergency entrance proceed directly to admissions and then to LDR suites. Obstetrical operating rooms for high-risk deliveries and C-sections, along with a 15-bay special-care nursery area, are located on the first floor.

As proposed in Nix Mann's original master plan for the complex, the Women's Pavilion is the first building to be located outside the campus loop road. A pedestrian bridge connects the pavilion with the existing hospital complex, providing linkage for patients and visitors and direct access for staff and support services housed within the hospital.

OPPOSITE:

On the Pavilion's second floor, postpartum rooms are arranged along the perimeter to provide new parents with individual rooms, which open onto private terraces.

RIGHT:

Mothers entering from the patient drop-off proceed directly to admissions and then to the LDR suites.

ABOVE:

The architects anchored the eastern end of the
Pavilion with an education/conference center,
defined with angled masonry walls and a large,
curving glass bay.

TOP:

The new Women's Pavilion, with its stepped volumes and varied roof lines, was designed as an individual element in the Gwinnett Medical Center landscape.

BOTTOM:

A glazed pedestrian bridge connects the new Pavilion with the existing hospital complex.

PROJECT LIST

AMBULATORY CARE/ OUTPATIENT CENTERS

The Johns Hopkins Outpatient Center *(pages 12-17)*

Baltimore, Maryland

Architects: Payette Associates, Boston

Engineers: Simpson Gumpertz & Heger (structural); Bard, Rao & Athanas/Sullivan Partnership (mechanical/electrical)

Photographer: Dan Forer

Shiley Eye Center, University of California, San Diego *(pages 18-21)*

San Diego, California

Architects: Anshen + Allen, San Francisco

Engineers: Ove Arup & Partners (structural); Rick Engineering (civil)

Photographers: David Hewitt/Anne Garrison; Mark Darley

Tang Center, United Health Services University of California, Berkeley *(pages 22-27)*

Berkeley, California

Architects: Anshen + Allen, San Francisco

Engineers: Foreli/Elsesser Engineers (structural/civil); Guttmann & MacRitchie (mechanical); The Engineering Enterprise (electrical)

Landscape Architects: Meacham O'Brien

Photographer: Beatriz Coll

University of Nebraska Medical Center, Outpatient Care Center *(pages 28-33)*

Omaha, Nebraska

Architects: Hansen Lind Meyer, Iowa City, Iowa

Associate Architects: Richard D. Nelson Company

Engineers: Hansen Lind Meyer

Photographer: Farshid Assassi

University of North Carolina Ambulatory Care Center *(pages 34-37)*

Chapel Hill, North Carolina

Architects: Ellerbe Becket, Washington, D.C.

Photographer: Ron Solomon

CANCER FACILITIES

Saint Francis Hospital Cancer Center *(pages 38-43)*

Hartford, Connecticut

Architects: TRO/The Ritchie Organization, Boston

Engineers: Hallisey & Hebert (structural)

Photographer: Warren Jagger

Sylvester Comprehensive Cancer Center, University of Miami School of Medicine *(pages 44-51)*

Miami, Florida

Architects: Payette Associates, Boston

Associate Architects: Baldwin Sackman Associates

Photographer: Dan Forer

Methodist Cancer Center, Nebraska Methodist Hospital *(pages 52-55)*

Omaha, Nebraska

Architects: HDR Inc., Omaha, Nebraska

Photographer: Tom Kessler

HEALTH MAINTENANCE ORGANIZATIONS

Kaiser Permanente Medical Campus *(pages 56-61)*

Fresno, California

Architects: The Ratcliff Architects, Berkeley, California

Associate Architects: Wiens/Carlstrom Architects

Engineers: Ove Arup & Partners (structural/mechanical/electrical)

Landscape Architect: Robert Boro

Photographer: Jane Lidz

Kaiser Permanente Medical Office Building *(pages 62-63)*

Vallejo, California

Architects: Skidmore, Owings & Merrill, New York

Photographer: Mark Darley/Esto

HOSPICES

Evergreen Hospice Center *(pages 64-67)*

Kirkland, Washington

Architects: Mahlum & Nordfors McKinley Gordon, Seattle, Washington
Engineers: ABKJ (structural); Sparling (electrical); Notkin Engineers (mechanical); Urban Design (landscape/civil)
Photographer: Robert Pisano

MEDICAL CENTERS

Central Washington Hospital *(pages 68-75)*
Wenatchee, Washington
    Architects: NBBJ, Seattle, Washington
    Engineers: Anderson Bjornstad Kane Jacobs (structural/civil); Hargis Engineers (mechanical); Sparling (electrical)
    Photographer: Paul Warchol

Columbus Regional Hospital *(pages 76-79)*
Columbus, Indiana
    Architects: Robert A. M. Stern Architects, New York
    Associate Architects: The Falick/Klein Partnership
    Landscape Architects: Robert A. M. Stern Architects
    Interior Design: Robert A. M. Stern Architects
    Engineers: Walter P. Moore & Associates (structural); Rotz Engineers (mechanical/electrical/plumbing)
    Photographer: Peter Aaron/Esto

Dartmouth-Hitchcock Medical Center *(pages 80-85)*
Lebanon, New Hampshire
    Architects: Shepley Bulfinch Richardson and Abbott, Boston
    Engineers: Souza True & Partners (structural); BR + A (mechanical/electrical); Robert W. Sullivan (plumbing)
    Landscape Architects: Peter G. Rolland & Associates
    Photographer: Jean M. Smith

Greater Baltimore Medical Center *(pages 86-89)*
Baltimore, Maryland
    Architects: RTKL, Baltimore, Maryland
    Engineers: Daft, McCune, Walker (civil/landscape); Walker Parking Consultants (parking)
    Photographer: Maxwell MacKenzie

McLaren Regional Medical Center *(pages 90-91)*
Flint, Michigan
    Architects: Perkins & Will, Chicago
    Photographer: Marco Lorenzetti/Hedrich-Blessing

New Boston City Hospital *(pages 92-95)*
Boston, Massachusetts
    Architects: Hoskins Scott & Partners/Cannon Architects, Boston
    Engineers: McNamara/Salvia (structural); BR + A (HVAC/electrical); Robert W. Sullivan (plumbing/fire protection); McPhail Associates (geotechnical); ASEC (civil)
    Photographer: R. Greg Hursley

St. Luke's Medical Tower *(pages 96-99)*
Houston, Texas
    Architects: Cesar Pelli & Associates, New Haven, Connecticut
    Associate Architects: Kendall Heaton Associates
    Interior Health Care Architects: Brooks/Collier
    Landscape Architects: The SWA Group
    Engineers: CBM Engineers (structural); I.A. Naman + Associates (mechanical/electrical); Walter P. Moore & Associates (civil)
    Photographer: Paul Hester

St. Luke's/Roosevelt Hospital Center *(pages 100-101)*
New York, New York
    Architects: Skidmore, Owings & Merrill, New York
    Associate Architects: Norman Rosenfeld Architects
    Interior Finishes: Perkins Eastman; Ed Mills
    Photographer: Wolfgang Hoyt

St. Vincent Hospital West Pavilion *(pages 102-105)*
Portland, Oregon
    Architects: Zimmer Gunsul Frasca Partnership, Portland, Oregon
    Engineers: Bouillon Christofferson & Schairer (mechanical/electrical); KPFF (structural/civil)
    Interiors: Karol Niemi Associates
    Landscape Architects: Murase Associates
    Photographer: Strode Eckert Photographic

South Pavilion, Roanoke
Memorial Hospital *(pages 106-109)*
Roanoke, Virginia
> **Architects:** JMGR Architects, Memphis, Tennessee
> **Engineers:** Newcomb & Boyd (mechanical/electrical); JMGR (structural); Mattern & Craig (civil); Schnabel Engineering (geotechnical)
> **Photographer:** Jeffrey Jacobs/MIM Studio

University of California,
San Diego Medical Center *(pages 110-115)*
San Diego, California
> **Architects:** Kaplan McLaughlin Diaz, San Francisco; Neptune-Thomas-Davis, San Diego, California
> **Landscape Architects:** KTU + A
> **Engineers:** Brandow & Johnston Associates (structural); Merle Strum & Associates (mechanical); Randall Lamb Associates (electrical); Barrett Consulting Group (civil)
> **Consultants:** Sussman/Prejza & Company (exterior colors and graphics)
> **Photographer:** David Hewitt/Anne Garrison

Health Central, West Orange Hospital *(pages 116-119)*
Ocoee, Florida
> **Architects:** HKS Inc., Dallas, Texas
> **Photographer:** Michael Lowry

Wilson Memorial Regional Medical Center,
United Health Services *(pages 120-123)*
Binghamton, New York
> **Architects:** Kaplan McLaughlin Diaz, San Francisco
> **Photographer:** Jeff Goldberg/Esto

MENTAL HEALTH FACILITIES

Acadia Hospital *(pages 124-127)*
Bangor, Maine
> **Architects:** Cannon Architects, Grand Island, New York
> **Photographer:** Brian Vanden Brink

Laurel Ridge Psychiatric Hospital *(pages 128-133)*
San Antonio, Texas
> **Architects:** HKS Inc., Dallas, Texas
> **Photographer:** R. Greg Hursley

John George Psychiatric Pavilion, Alameda County
Department of Health Services *(pages 134-137)*
San Leandro, California
> **Architects:** The Ratcliff Architects, Berkeley, California
> **Program Consultant Architects:** The Design Partnership, San Francisco
> **Engineers:** Graham & Kellam Engineers (structural); Buonaccorsi & Associates (mechanical); PLS (electrical)
> **Landscape Architects:** Haygood & Associates
> **Photographer:** Jane Lidz

PEDIATRIC FACILITIES

Children's Hospital and Health Center *(pages 138-143)*
San Diego, California
> **Architects:** NBBJ, Seattle, Washington
> **Engineers:** Willis-McNaughton & Associates (structural); Rick Engineering (civil); GEM (mechanical); Brown-Zammitt Engineering (electrical)
> **Landscape Architects:** KTU + A
> **Photographer:** David Hewitt/Anne Garrison

Children's Hospital at
Yale New Haven Hospital *(pages 144-147)*
New Haven, Connecticut
> **Architects:** Shepley Bulfinch Richardson and Abbott, Boston
> **Engineers:** Spiegel Zamecnik & Shah (structural); BR + A (mechanical/electrical); Robert W. Sullivan (plumbing/fire protection)
> **Interior Finishes and Coordination:** Rosalyn Cama Design Associates
> **Landscape Architects:** Rolland/Towers
> **Photographer:** Peter Aaron/Esto

The Hospital for Sick Children *(pages 148-151)*

Toronto, Ontario

    Architects: Zeidler Roberts Partnership, Toronto, Ontario

    Engineers: Quinn Dressel Associates (structural); ECE Group (mechanical/electrical)

    Landscape Architects: Baker Salmona Associates

    Photographer: Balthazar Korab

Hospital for Sick Children *(pages 152-157)*

Washington, D.C.

    Architects for Exterior of Building: Weinstein Associates Architects, Washington, DC

    Architects of Record: Herbert Cohen & Associates

    Interior Design: RTKL

    Photographers: Maxwell MacKenzie (exteriors); William Lebovich (interiors)

**Kirk Scharfenberg House
for Children with AIDS** *(pages 158-159)*

Mattapan, Massachusetts

    Architects: Buck, Smith & McAvoy, Boston

    Interiors: Boston Interior Design Community

    Photographer: David Foster

Shriners' Hospital for Crippled Children *(pages 160-163)*

Minneapolis, Minnesota

    Architects: Odell Associates, Charlotte, North Carolina

    Photographer: Tim Buchman

REHABILITATION CENTERS

**Rehabcentre, South Fulton
Medical Center** *(pages 164-165)*

East Point, Georgia

    Architects: Nix Mann and Associates, Atlanta, Georgia

    Photographer: Gary Knight

**Shenandoah Regional Center,
Learning Services Corporation** *(pages 166-173)*

Manassas, Virginia

    Architects: Richard Rauh & Associates, Atlanta, Georgia

    Engineers: Jack Lynch & Associates (structural); Jones Nall & Davis (mechanical/electrical); RBA Group, Kidde Consultants (civil)

    Owner's Representative: Clarence Bradshaw

    Photographers: Peter Mauss/Esto; Maxwell MacKenzie

WOMEN'S HEALTH CENTERS

**Orchard Pavilion, Maternal and Child Health Center,
El Camino Hospital** *(pages 174-177)*

Mountain View, California

    Architects: Lee Burkhart Liu, Santa Monica, California

    Engineers: KPFF (structural); Rosenberg Associates (mechanical); Cohen & Kanwar (electrical)

    Photographers: Steve Wittaker; Morgan J. Cowin

**Women's Center, Pomona Valley Hospital
and Medical Center** *(pages 178-183)*

Pomona, California

    Architects: NBBJ, Seattle, Washington

    Engineers: Taylor & Gaines (structural); Popov Engineering (mechanical/electrical/plumbing)

    Photographer: Paul Warchol

**Women's Pavilion,
Gwinnett Medical Center** *(pages 184-187)*

Lawrenceville, Georgia

    Architects: Nix Mann and Associates, Atlanta, Georgia

    Photographer: Timothy Hursley